Those Who Are
DANGEROUS
SONS

DAG HEWARD-MILLS

Parchment House

Unless otherwise stated, all Scripture quotations are taken from the King James Version of the Bible.

Copyright © 2011 Dag Heward-Mills

Originally published under the title *Fathers and Loyalty*
by Parchment House 2011

ISBN: 978-9988-8500-1-2

This edition published 2014 by Parchment House
3rd Printing 2014

Find out more about Dag Heward-Mills at:

Healing Jesus Campaign
Write to: evangelist@daghewardmills.org
Website: www.daghewardmills.org
Facebook: Dag Heward-Mills
Twitter: @EvangelistDag

ISBN: 978-9988-8572-0-2

Contents

Chapter 1

How to Identify a Father

For though ye have ten thousand instructors in Christ, yet have ye NOT MANY FATHERS: for in Christ Jesus I have begotten you through the gospel.

1 Corinthians 4:15

The gift of a "father" is a rare gift. Not every man of God is a father. Not everyone who teaches the Word of God is a father. Not all the visiting preachers and teachers were fathers.

Not every prophet is father and Paul pointed this out to the Corinthians.

A Father Is a Rare Gift

There will be many people who will make an input into your life. Instructors and teachers abound but these are different from fathers. A father's input is comprehensive. A father gives you a complete package that goes further than a good teaching. A teacher is concerned about giving a good lesson. A prophet is concerned about ministering the power of God through visions, dreams and words of knowledge. But a father is concerned with your total welfare.

Because fathering involves much more, there are not many fathers! It is easier to go through the prepared notes than it is to give total care. People can be so difficult and so ungrateful that only fathers can handle them over the long term.

There are many, many pastors, evangelists and prophets, but a fathering prophet – who can find? That is why Paul said: "You can have ten thousand instructors but you do not have many fathers."

The key characteristic of a father is not his age but his ability to produce after his own kind. Contrary to some opinions, there are many young people with a father's heart.

In the natural, people often become fathers at a young age. The proof of fatherhood is in *the children* who are produced by the father. It takes love, commitment and patience to bring up children. In the end, *the children* attest to your fatherhood.

If you compare the ministries of Elijah and Elisha, for instance, you will find the differences between a fathering prophet and a non-fathering prophet. These differences become quite clear when you study their ministries. By comparing the ministries of Elijah and Elisha, you quickly see the differences between a man who has a father's heart and one who does not.

Both Elijah and Elisha were excellent prophets. But Elijah had an additional gift of being a father. That is why he had a successor. Elisha had no successor. He cursed Gehazi who was next in line to him. He cursed Gehazi when he made a mistake with money. The father's heart does not curse his only child.

The fathering spirit is that thing which causes a man of God to produce people just like himself in the ministry. Very simply put, the fathering gift is a manifestation of God's love. It takes love to bring up people who don't understand what is being done for them.

It takes love to bring up people who will not understand you for many years. Truly, God sends many, many teachers who minister to our lives. They will minister the lessons and the points that make up the doctrine. But a father will go many steps further. *In addition to teaching you, he will minister the love and the patience that are needed to bring you into God's perfect will.*

Idealism in a minister makes him look for perfection all the time. Idealists and perfectionists are not usually good fathers. They often do not appreciate that the grace of God is working slowly in someone's life. They insist on perfection all the time and that is not possible with human beings.

You can receive a man of God as a teacher. You can also receive him as a pastor. You may receive a man of God as a prophet or evangelist. It is also possible to receive him as a father.

May you find a father in this life! May you receive the capacity to love and to become a father yourself!

Chapter 2

How to Recognize and Receive Different Fathers at the Different Seasons of Life

God will send you different fathers at different times.

For though ye have ten thousand instructors in Christ, yet have ye not many fathers: for in Christ Jesus I have begotten you through the gospel.

1 Corinthians 4:15

God is going to send a number of different people to father you. The first of these is your earthly father whom you must receive properly. You must not see your earthly father as an "ancient of days" who is out of touch with the realities of modern life. Seeing your biological father as outmoded hinders you from receiving his great wisdom.

This biological father will have his limitations in fathering. Soon the relay will have to begin and the next person sent by the Lord to father you will arrive on the scene. Through his ministry, you will receive the fatherly care that you need to go through the next stage of your life. Then another person may arise who will play a fatherly role in your life. A relay of sorts is in motion! The baton of fatherhood has passed from one person to the other.

There are many things that your biological father doesn't talk to you about. Maybe he should talk about everything, but he doesn't. For many of us, our parents did not give us step by step counselling on choosing a wife or a husband. Most biological parents just made comments about different things in marriage.

That is often as far as their marriage counselling goes. Thank God for the pastors who often take up that role and guide children into marriage. Pastors often become the next father in the relay.

One day, my daughter asked me a question, "Daddy, how do people become pregnant?"

I was taken aback by the question but I answered, "God makes them pregnant."

But she insisted, "I know God makes them pregnant but how does it happen?"

I mumbled some answer and managed to change the topic.

Later my wife said to me, "You have to talk to your children about sex."

I answered, "Why should I? *You* talk to them about it."

We began to argue and she said, "You are the head of the house so you are the one who must talk to them."

But I answered, "You are their mother and you are always talking to them, so why don't you talk to them about this as well?"

She continued, "It is your duty and you must play your role!"

But I didn't agree. I used my authority as the head of the house and delegated her to talk to the children about all these things.

You see, we had reached the place where our fathering and mothering abilities were wavering. We wished that God would send others to minister to our children as we had ministered to other people's children. We were praying that the next father in the relay would appear on the scene and help guide the children to safety.

Among the hundreds of instructors and teachers, it is always important to recognize who the fathers are. Fathers have a wider scope of concern for your life. Their input goes beyond even what they say. You will discover that their ministry cares for you totally. Their ministry has an uncanny wide-ranging effect on your life.

One of the keys to recognizing a father is to recognize the love, care and direction of our Heavenly Father being transmitted through him to your life.

Many people mistakenly think that the verse says you have ten thousand teachers but you have one father. The Scripture says that you do not have many fathers. It says in other words that you have a few fathers.

Jesus said, "Don't call anyone father."

And call no man your father upon the earth: for one is your Father, which is in heaven.

Matthew 23:9

This is because no human being could truly be all that a father is supposed to be. All men fall short of this role and only the Heavenly Father truly exemplifies what a father is.

Have you not noticed how earthly fathers often compete and fight with their children? Even biological fathers can inflict a lot of pain and suffering on their children.

Many people hate their fathers. And there are many whose lives are distorted because of their fathers. This is ample evidence that fathering by the natural man is fraught with imperfections.

This is the reason why there is a need for what I call, "the relay of the fathers".

The relay involves God sending one person after another for different phases of your life and ministry. It is important to recognize the different people as they walk into your life.

This is what Jesus was illustrating with the parable in Matthew 21. Indeed we will be judged by the way we receive the different fathers God sends to us.

Hear another parable: There was a certain householder, which planted a vineyard, and hedged it round about, and digged a winepress in it, and built

a tower, and let it out to husbandmen, and went into a far country: and when the time of the fruit drew near, he SENT HIS SERVANTS to the husbandmen, that they might receive the fruits of it.

And the husbandmen took his servants, and beat one, and killed another, and stoned another. Again, he SENT OTHER SERVANTS more than the first: and they did unto them likewise.

But last of all he sent unto them his son, saying, They will reverence my son. But when the husbandmen saw the son, they said among themselves, This is the heir; come, let us kill him, and let us seize on his inheritance.

And they caught him, and cast him out of the vineyard, and slew him.

Matthew 21:33-39

God sends fathers into our lives whom we often do not recognize. People even fight with their fathers! We must learn to receive the fathers God sends into our lives.

What Is the Difference between Receiving a Father and Receiving an Instructor?

Receiving an instructor involves receiving the lessons he gives from the Word. Receiving a father involves receiving someone in such a way that a vital life-giving ministry will come to you.

In the natural, your biological father affects you in many ways. He teaches you how to eat, how to dress and how to live. He gives you wisdom, advice and little lessons for life. He sets an example for you to follow and serves as a source of inspiration and direction.

Compare this with your school teachers. These instructors often do not guide as comprehensively as fathers do. When you come across someone who has a wide-ranging influence on your life, you have probably met one of the fathers God has ordained for you.

Don't Make the Mistake of Receiving a Father as a Mere Instructor

Some people make the mistake of receiving their fathers as mere teachers. They do this by not embracing all the fatherly input coming their way. By receiving only a part of the input of these fathers, we often reduce the role of fathers to mere instructors. There are people God has called me to father. But I relate with them as an instructor because that is what they want.

The parable in Matthew, Chapter 21, clearly shows that God will judge us for the way we relate to the people He sends us. There are fathers that God has sent to me.

One day, I was enjoying a message by a man of God when the Lord spoke to me. He said, "I sent this man to you as a father. I want you to receive him as a father from now on." From that moment onwards, I regarded those tapes differently.

I opened my heart to receive all aspects of the ministry that were offered to me through this minister.

Suddenly, this person's books and CDs were of greater interest to me. At first, I just enjoyed some of his teachings but now I wanted everything. I knew that I was to be birthed into a new level of ministry through this man.

That was really when I understood that you can receive someone as an instructor but then you can go higher and receive him as a father.

Chapter 3

Ten Types of Fathers

1. Your Heavenly Father

...When ye pray, say, Our Father which art in heaven...

Luke 11:2

Most of us have the impression that the Heavenly Father is an angry God who would have burnt us all up, if it had not been for the intervention of Christ. We often have **the feeling that He still wants to burn us!**

God is filled with indescribable love. Our Heavenly Father cares for us. A close look at the story of the prodigal son shows the attitude of the Father towards His sinful children. He loves us. Although we sin a thousand times, He still loves us.

And he arose, and came to his father. But when he was yet a great way off, his father saw him, and had compassion, and ran, and fell on his neck, and kissed him. And the son said unto him, Father, I have sinned against heaven, and in thy sight, and am no more worthy to be called thy son. But the father said to his servants, Bring forth the best robe, and put it on him; and put a ring on his hand, and shoes on his feet: And bring hither the fatted calf, and kill it; and let us eat, and be merry: For this my son was dead, and is alive again; he was lost, and is found. And they began to be merry.

Luke 15:20-24

2. Your Father in Christ

This is the person who brought you to the Lord. He or she is the one through whom you gave your life to Christ and became a born-again Christian. God sends people to us who birth us into

9

the Lord. We must always cherish and honour them. It is because of them that we will one day go to Heaven.

3. Your Spiritual Father

This is the person who trains you in spiritual things. The one who leads you to Christ may not bring you up spiritually. Your spiritual father will train you to have your quiet time with the Lord. A spiritual father will introduce you to the habits that would make you a spiritual giant. A spiritual father may introduce you to other Christian friends. A spiritual father may introduce you to good churches and fellowships. A spiritual father may pray for you to receive the baptism of the Holy Spirit. A spiritual father may teach you basic things from the Word that will help you stand up for Christ.

4. Your Father in the Ministry

Often, *fathers in ministry* are confused with *fathers in Christ* and spiritual fathers. People generally refer to fathers in ministry as spiritual fathers. But a *father in Christ* is very different from a *father in ministry* or a spiritual father. A father in Christ births you into Jesus Christ and a father in ministry births you into the work of ministry.

God has blessed me with wonderful men of God through whom my life has been totally transformed. I have become a pastor and a minister through their fathering grace. In recent times, the Lord has blessed me by sending another father to lift me into the next phase of ministry.

A father in ministry is the person who birthed you into the ministry of the Lord. Through him you find yourself involved in the most important work in the world.

5. Your Biological Father

This is the father from whose seed you were born. This person is often the only one who receives the recognition of a father. This is a great mistake because he is not and cannot be the only one who fathers you. That is why Jesus said, "Call no man your father!" He knew that no earthly person could single-handedly father anyone.

And call no man your father upon the earth: for one is your Father, which is in heaven.

Matthew 23:9

I always pray that God will send fathers into the lives of my children to help them at different stages of their lives.

One day I was praying for some young people at a revival. I prayed for them with all my heart. Then it struck me: "Will there be somebody to pray for my daughter when she is twenty-one years old?"

I prayed that God would send people into the lives of my children so that they would be blessed and cared for at the different stages of their lives.

6. Your Substitute Father

Sometimes, biological fathers are not available because they are dead, divorced or have simply abandoned their children. Many people grow up in non-ideal situations and God raises people to do the work of fathering.

One day, I stood in grief over the dead body of one of my pastors. I was holding his trembling wife, desperately trying to console her as she looked at her dead husband's body. Shortly after this, one of the doctors on the ward spoke to me. I will never forget what he said.

He said to me, "Don't worry. I know you will be thinking: 'Why did he die? Why should such a good person leave us now?' "

He continued, "People will say, 'God must be angry with the church for a pastor to die. '"

He went on, "But you see, death is part of life. We do not understand everything that God does."

Then he said something that surprised me, "My father died at the age of twenty-five when I was in my mother's womb."

He said, "It must have been very sad for my mother. I never saw my own father."

He continued, "Perhaps I would not have become a world famous surgeon if my biological father had lived."

This man had become a world-class surgeon and was greatly respected all over the nation. He had achieved this great feat, not through the help of a biological father, but through the help of a "substitute" father.

A substitute father is someone who steps in to father a child when the real father is not around. Sometimes, substitute fathers are even better than biological fathers. There are two lessons we can learn from this:

Don't be afraid to die. God will take care of your children. He will raise up substitute fathers who may be even better fathers than you are.

Don't hold back love if you have a chance to adopt a child or care for somebody's child. You may be the substitute father that God is raising to care for a fatherless child.

7. Your Father-in-Law

Now Moses kept the flock of Jethro his father in law, the priest of Midian: and he led the flock to the backside of the desert, and came to the mountain of God, even to Horeb.

Exodus 3:1

Your father-in-law is another important father. Moses was greatly blessed through his father-in-law. He received important advice through his father-in-law.

My father-in-law has been a great blessing to me. He inspired me to be debt free and to become a builder. Indeed, God used

12

my father-in-law to bless my life. There are many times I have pointed out to my wife how blessed she is to have such a father.

8. The Father of a Church

The father of a church is the founder of the church. He is the father in the sense that he gave birth to the church. Through his ministry, the church came into existence. Like Paul said to the Corinthians, "I have begotten you (given birth to you) through the gospel."

For though ye have ten thousand instructors in Christ, yet have ye not many fathers: for in Christ Jesus I have begotten you through the gospel.

1 Corinthians 4:15

9. The Father of a Movement

Know ye therefore that they which are of faith, the same are the children of Abraham.

Galatians 3:7

There are also fathers of movements. For example, Abraham is seen as the father of faith. Such people are recognized as those who give birth to generations.

Kenneth Hagin is seen as the father of the modern Faith Movement.

John Wesley is the father of the Methodist Church Movement.

Fathers are special. Sons may do greater works than fathers, but they are still not recognized as fathers. For instance, in the ministry today, there are great healers and pastors, but the fathers always stand out as fathers.

Elisha did greater works than Elijah did. Elisha's miracles were often twice as powerful as Elijah's and he did twice as many miracles as Elijah did.

Joshua entered the Promised Land. He conquered a land which Moses was unable to enter. He accomplished Moses' dream with a great display of power. But neither Elisha nor Joshua had a successor. They were great ministers but not fathers.

On the mount of transfiguration, neither Elisha nor Joshua was present with Jesus. The fathers were those who appeared in the vision.

Never forget that fathers are special to the Lord. Young people should not be deceived by their accomplishments. Do not think that you are greater than your father! All that sons and daughters do is to build upon the advances already made by fathers.

10. Your Father in Sin

A father in sin is the one who introduces you to the life of sin.

Some of us would never have known the depths of sin if it had not been for those who virtually took our hands and led us into evil.

Some of us would never have known about fornication if we had not met certain people who trained us in sexual sin.

Chapter 4

Seven Reasons Why Problems Pass from Fathers to Sons

Be careful how you criticize your daddy because the devils that fought your daddy will one day fight you. They are just waiting for you to grow up.

Whether you like it or not, one day, you will have to fight "your daddy's devil".

One man of God said to me, "People want to retire me! They want me to be removed from my position in this nation. They think I have too many problems."

He said something I will not easily forget: "When I am gone, the 'thing' that was fighting me will begin to fight them."

This is an eternal principle and it will be wise to grow up and understand it quickly. Many sons have had to swallow their words as they walked into their father's footsteps and made the exact same mistakes. Notice how this happened with Abraham, Isaac, Jacob, David, and Solomon.

A son who criticizes his father usually inherits his father's problems *and* devils. Being critical of a person opens you up to the person's problems for a number of reasons.

Seven Reasons Why Problems Can Pass from Fathers to Sons

1. **Problems pass from fathers to the sons who murmur and criticize.**

   Murmuring and criticizing is a sin and sins open the door to evil spirits.

   Evil spirits operate in the darkness of sin. There are sons who criticize their father and pay heavily for it.

The evil spirit of incurable sickness attached itself to Miriam when she criticized Moses.

The evil spirit of death and destruction fell upon the Israelites when they murmured against Moses. None of them passed into the Promised Land.

Similarly, the spirit of demotion, affliction, inferiority and mediocrity came upon Ham when he despised his father. Noah was disgraced and embarrassed by the exposure of his nakedness. But now, Ham and his descendants would be disgraced and embarrassed by the mediocrity of their lives.

And MIRIAM AND AARON SPAKE AGAINST MOSES because of the Ethiopian woman whom he had married: for he had married an Ethiopian woman.

And they said, Hath the LORD indeed spoken only by Moses? Hath he not spoken also by us? And the LORD heard *it*.

(Now the man Moses was very meek, above all the men which were upon the face of the earth.)

And the LORD spake suddenly unto Moses, and unto Aaron, and unto Miriam, Come out ye three unto the tabernacle of the congregation. And they three came out.

And the LORD came down in the pillar of the cloud, and stood *in* the door of the tabernacle, and called Aaron and Miriam: and they both came forth.

And he said, Hear now my words: If there be a prophet among you, *I* the LORD will make myself known unto him in a vision, *and* will speak unto him in a dream.

My servant Moses *is* not so, who *is* faithful in all mine house.

With him will I speak mouth to mouth, even apparently, and not in dark speeches; and the similitude of the LORD shall he behold: wherefore then were ye not afraid to speak against my servant Moses?

And the anger of the LORD was kindled against them; and he departed.

And the cloud departed from off the tabernacle; and, behold, MIRIAM *BECAME* LEPROUS, *WHITE* AS SNOW: and Aaron looked upon Miriam, and, behold, *she* was leprous.

Numbers 12:1-10

2. Problems pass from fathers to the sons who mock at their fathers and bring upon themselves a curse.

Mocking a father attracts a well-known biblical curse in which birds pluck out the eyes of children.

There are sons who mock at their fathers. Even having a despising attitude brings a curse. A son who despises his father should expect certain curses to be fulfilled in his life. A son can inherit curses that will give rise to his father's problems and *more*. Children who despise their fathers are simply cursed!

The eye *that* mocketh at *his* father, and despiseth to obey *his* mother, the ravens of the valley shall pick it out, and the young eagles shall eat it.

Proverbs 30:17

3. Problems pass from fathers to the sons who despise the advice of their fathers. Despising the advice of a father makes you a fool.

There are sons who despise the advice of their fathers and that makes them fools. Being a fool gives you many painful strokes in this life.

Read it for yourself: "A fool despiseth his father's instruction: but he that regardeth reproof is prudent" (Proverbs 15:5). "... a foolish man despiseth his mother" (Proverbs 15:20). Becoming a fool causes you to receive strokes in life. If you had not despised your father you would not have received those strokes. Many of the sad experiences of your life are the strokes that you are receiving for despising your father and mother. You will also notice that many of the strokes you get are the strokes that your father got in his time.

A fool's lips enter into contention, and HIS MOUTH CALLETH FOR STROKES.

Proverbs 18:6

4. **Problems pass from fathers to sons because of the pride in their sons.**

It is only when you feel you are as good as someone that you criticize the person. A humble person does not speak great swelling words of pride. When sons begin to have arguments with their fathers, they reveal how big and proud they have become. Only by pride comes contention (Proverbs 13:10).

Pride comes before a fall. Pride in the sons comes before the fall of the sons. The mistakes of fathers stir up the critical spirit of proud children.

They speak heatedly and angrily about the person who brought them into existence and made them who they are. They criticize what they do not understand and this spirit of pride opens the door for their own destruction.

Pride *goeth* before destruction, and an haughty spirit before a fall.

Proverbs 16:18

5. **Problems pass from fathers to the sons because of the blindness of the sons.**

When you are blind you cannot see any good thing in your father. Blindness is the affliction that strikes critical people. There are sons who are blinded because they despise and dishonour their fathers. The blindness of the son is caused by their lack of respect. Blindness comes about when people casually dismiss the importance of their fathers. As they dismiss the relevance of their fathers, they are unable to perceive his wisdom; they are unable to learn from his experiences, and they are unable to understand why he made the mistakes he did. They do not see or understand his trials and difficulties. Because of this, they set themselves up to walk in exactly the same path.

The eye *that* mocketh at *his* father, and despiseth to obey *his* mother, the ravens of the valley shall pick it out, and the young eagles shall eat it.

Proverbs 30:17

6. Problems pass from fathers to the sons because they do not take their fathers' words seriously.

Despising your father will cause you not to take his words seriously. The Bible describes this as 'not holding fast to his words in your life'. Many sons do not pay attention to details when their fathers are trying to teach them something. When he explains why certain problems exist they do not take them seriously. Notice how Solomon urged his son to pay attention to the things he was saying.

> When I was a son to my father, Tender and the only son in the sight of my mother,
>
> Then he taught me and said to me, "LET YOUR HEART HOLD FAST MY WORDS; Keep my commandments and live;
>
> Acquire wisdom! Acquire understanding! Do not forget, nor turn away from the words of my mouth.
>
> "Do not forsake her, and she will guard you; Love her, and she will watch over you.
>
> "The beginning of wisdom is: Acquire wisdom; And with all your acquiring, get understanding.
>
> "Prize her, and she will exalt you; She will honor you if you embrace her.
>
> "She will place on your head a garland of grace; She will present you with a crown of beauty."
>
> Hear, my son, and accept my sayings, And the years of your life will be many.

Proverbs 4:3-10 (NASB)

7. **Problems pass from fathers to the sons who do not recognize and honour the great men who are given to them as fathers.**

Desolation will happen to men who do not recognize the great men who are given to them as fathers. Desolation is predicted for those who do not recognize the greatness of the people sent to them. People have great men as their fathers but do not recognize them. Instead of honouring them they kill them. This is exactly what happened to Jesus.

O Jerusalem, Jerusalem, which killest the prophets, and stonest them that sent unto thee; how often would I have gathered thy children together, as a hen *doth gather* her brood under her wings, and ye would not!

Behold, YOUR HOUSE IS LEFT UNTO YOU DESOLATE: and verily I say unto you, Ye shall not see me, until *the time* come when ye shall say, Blessed *is* he that cometh in the name of the Lord."

Luke 13:34-35

Chapter 5

Sons Who Inherited Problems

A study of the lives of different sons and their fathers reveals an uncanny pattern of repetition. You would wonder why the sons are falling into the exact same problems of their fathers. History teaches us that people do not learn from history! Unfortunately, many sons are cut off from the lessons their fathers learnt. Many sons dismiss the problems their fathers had as being peculiar to them. Advice is given but it is not heeded. Many sons simply do not pay attention to the lessons being transmitted by their fathers.

The result of this flippant attitude is a repetition of the calamities and catastrophes of the fathers by the sons. The Bible shows us how Abraham disowned his wife. He told King Abimelech of Gerar that she was his sister and thereby disowned her. Many years later, his son Isaac did exactly the same thing.

King David had big problems in his life and ministry because he slept with somebody's wife. His sons ruined their lives by doing exactly the same things. Amnon may have been angry with his father David for having an affair with Bathsheba. But he ended up raping his own sister Tamar.

Absalom may have been angry with his father David for sleeping with Bathsheba. He may have been angry with his father David for not punishing Amnon for the rape of Tamar. David's failure in these areas may have sparked off the rebellion in Absalom. But in the end Absalom himself ended up sleeping with all his father's wives.

Solomon also had his life destroyed by his interaction with women. You would have thought that Solomon would learn from the mistakes of his father. Perhaps he did. Perhaps he decided that he would marry any woman he felt attracted to. In the end he married over a thousand women. Solomon's problems with women became even more complicated because they led him away from Jehovah. It is sad to say that Solomon ended up as an idol worshipper. May God deliver the sons from the blindness that makes them walk headlong into the difficulties their fathers had.

1.   ABRAHAM AND HIS SON ISAAC

How Abraham Disowned His Wife

And Abraham journeyed from thence toward the south country, and dwelled between Kadesh and Shur, and sojourned in Gerar.

And Abraham said of Sarah his wife, SHE IS MY SISTER: and Abimelech king of Gerar sent, and took Sarah. "But God came to Abimelech in a dream by night, and said to him, Behold, thou art but a dead man, for the woman which thou hast taken; for she is a man's wife.

But Abimelech had not come near her: and he said, Lord, wilt thou slay also a righteous nation?

Said he not unto me, SHE IS MY SISTER? and she, even she herself said, He is my brother: in the integrity of my heart and innocency of my hands have I done this.

And God said unto him in a dream, Yea, I know that thou didst this in the integrity of thy heart; for I also withheld thee from sinning against me: therefore suffered I thee not to touch her.

Now therefore restore the man his wife; for he is a prophet, and he shall pray for thee, and thou shalt live: and if thou restore her not, know thou that thou shalt surely die, thou, and all that are thine.

Genesis 20:1-7

How Isaac Disowned His Wife

And there was a famine in the land, beside the first famine that was in the days of Abraham. And Isaac went unto Abimelech king of the Philistines unto Gerar.

And the LORD appeared unto him, and said, Go not down into Egypt; dwell in the land which I shall tell thee of:

Sojourn in this land, and I will be with thee, and will bless thee; for unto thee, and unto thy seed, I will give all these countries, and I will perform the oath which I sware unto Abraham thy father;

And I will make thy seed to multiply as the stars of heaven, and will give unto thy seed all these countries; and in thy seed shall all the nations of the earth be blessed;

Because that Abraham obeyed my voice, and kept my charge, my commandments, my statutes, and my laws.

And Isaac dwelt in Gerar:

And the men of the place asked *him* of his wife; and he said, She *is* my sister: for he feared to say, *She is* my wife; lest, *said he*, the men of the place should kill me for Rebekah; because she *was* fair to look upon.

And it came to pass, when he had been there a long time, that Abimelech king of the Philistines looked out at a window, and saw, and, behold, Isaac was sporting with Rebekah his wife.

And Abimelech called Isaac, and said, Behold, of a surety she *is* thy wife: and how saidst thou, She is my sister? And Isaac said unto him, Because I said, Lest I die for her.

And Abimelech said, What is this thou hast done unto us? one of the people might lightly have lien with thy wife, and thou shouldest have brought guiltiness upon us.

And Abimelech charged all *his* people, saying, He that toucheth this man or his wife shall surely be put to death.

Genesis 26:1-11

2. DAVID AND HIS SONS AMNON, ABSALOM AND SOLOMON

How David had Problems with Women

And it came to pass in an eveningtide, that David arose from off his bed, and walked upon the roof of the king's house: and from the roof he saw a woman washing herself; and the woman was very beautiful to look upon. And David sent messengers, and took her; and she came in unto him, and he lay with her; for she was purified from her uncleanness: and she returned unto her house.

2 Samuel 11:2,4

How Amnon had Problems with Women

And it came to pass after this, that Absalom the son of David had a fair sister, whose name *was* Tamar; and Amnon the son of David loved her.

And Amnon was so vexed, that he fell sick for his sister Tamar; for she *was* a virgin; and Amnon thought it hard for him to do any thing to her.

But Amnon had a friend, whose name *was* Jonadab, the son of Shimeah David's brother: and Jonadab *was* a very subtil man.

And he said unto him, Why *art* thou, *being* the king's son, lean from day to day? wilt thou not tell me? And Amnon said unto him, I love Tamar, my brother Absalom's sister.

And Jonadab said unto him, Lay thee down on thy bed, and make thyself sick: and when thy father cometh to see thee, say unto him, I pray thee, let my sister Tamar come, and give me meat, and dress the meat in my sight, that I may see *it*, and eat *it* at her hand.

So Amnon lay down, and made himself sick: and when the king was come to see him, Amnon said unto the king, I pray thee, let Tamar my sister come, and make me a couple of cakes in my sight, that I may eat at her hand.

Then David sent home to Tamar, saying, Go now to thy brother Amnon's house, and dress him meat.

So Tamar went to her brother Amnon's house; and he was laid down. And she took flour, and kneaded *it*, and made cakes in his sight, and did bake the cakes.

And she took a pan, and poured *them* out before him; but he refused to eat. And Amnon said, Have out all men from me. And they went out every man from him.

And Amnon said unto Tamar, Bring the meat into the chamber, that I may eat of thine hand. And Tamar took the cakes which she had made, and brought *them* into the chamber to Amnon her brother.

And when she had brought *them* unto him to eat, he took hold of her, and said unto her, Come lie with me, my sister.

And she answered him, Nay, my brother, do not force me; for no such thing ought to be done in Israel: do not thou this folly.

And I, whither shall I cause my shame to go? and as for thee, thou shalt be as one of the fools in Israel. Now therefore, I pray thee, speak unto the king; for he will not withhold me from thee.

Howbeit he would not hearken unto her voice: but, being stronger than she, forced her, and lay with her.

Then Amnon hated her exceedingly; so that the hatred wherewith he hated her was greater than the love wherewith he had loved her. And Amnon said unto her, Arise, be gone.

2 Samuel 13:1-15

How Absalom had Problems with Women

Then Absalom turned to Ahithophel and asked him, "What should I do next?"

Ahithophel told him, "Go and sleep with your father's concubines, for he has left them here to keep the house. Then all Israel will know that you have insulted him beyond hope of reconciliation, and they will give you their support."

So they set up a tent on the palace roof where everyone could see it, and Absalom went into the tent to sleep with his father's concubines.

Absalom followed Ahithophel's advice, just as David had done. For every word Ahithophel spoke seemed as wise as though it had come directly from the mouth of God.

2 Samuel 16:20-23 (NLT)

How Solomon had Problems with Women

But king SOLOMON LOVED MANY STRANGE WOMEN, together with the daughter of Pharaoh, women of the Moabites, Ammonites, Edomites, Zidonians, *and* Hittites;

Of the nations *concerning* which the LORD said unto the children of Israel, Ye shall not go in to them, neither shall they come in unto you: *for* surely they will turn away your heart after their gods: Solomon clave unto these in love.

And he had seven hundred wives, princesses, and three hundred concubines: AND HIS WIVES TURNED AWAY HIS HEART.

1 Kings 11:1-3

3. ABRAHAM, HIS SON ISAAC AND GRANDSON JACOB

How Abraham Set Aside His First-Born Son

And Abraham rose up early in the morning, and took bread, and a bottle of water, and gave it unto Hagar, putting it on her shoulder, and the child, and sent her away: and she departed, and wandered in the wilderness of Beer-sheba.

Genesis 21:14

How Isaac Set Aside His First-Born Son

And it came to pass, as soon as ISAAC HAD MADE AN END OF BLESSING JACOB, and Jacob was yet scarce gone out from the presence of Isaac his father, that Esau his brother came in from his hunting.

And he also had made savoury meat, and brought it unto his father, and said unto his father, Let my father arise, and eat of his son's venison, that thy soul may bless me.

And Isaac his father said unto him, Who *art* thou? And he said, I am thy son, thy firstborn Esau.

And Isaac trembled very exceedingly, and said, Who? where *is* he that hath taken venison, and brought it me, and I have eaten of all before thou camest, and have blessed him? yea, *and* he shall be blessed.

And when Esau heard the words of his father, he cried with a great and exceeding bitter cry, and said unto his father, Bless me, *even* me also, O my father.

And he said, Thy brother came with subtilty, and hath taken away thy blessing.

And he said, Is not he rightly named Jacob? for he hath supplanted me these two times: he took away my birthright; and, behold, now he hath taken away my blessing. And he said, Hast thou not reserved a blessing for me?

And Isaac answered and said unto Esau, Behold, I have made him thy lord, and all his brethren have I given to him for servants; and with corn and wine have I sustained him: and what shall I do now unto thee, my son?

Genesis 27:30-37

How Jacob Set Aside His First-Born Son

Then Jacob called together all his sons and said, "Gather around me, and I will tell you what is going to happen to you in the days to come.

"Come and listen, O sons of Jacob; listen to Israel, your father.

"Reuben, you are my oldest son, the child of my vigorous youth. You are first on the list in rank and honor.

But you are as unruly as the waves of the sea, and you will be first no longer. For you slept with one of my wives; you dishonored me in my own bed."

Genesis 49:1-4 (NLT)

Chapter 6

Seven Signs of a True Son

One day, a couple sat before me at the counselling table. The lady said to me, "Oh Bishop, I am your daughter." But I corrected her and said, "You are not my daughter, you are just a church member."

She looked hurt but I continued, "You are a very nice church member who is always smiling around and encouraging us but that doesn't make you a daughter. You are a VNP but you are not a daughter."

There are five types of church members: very nice people (VNPs), very encouraging people (VEPs), very important people (VIPs), very significant people (VSPs) and very dangerous people (VDPs).

I went on to explain:

I asked her, "When you see my children running around in the church, how do you know that they are my children?"

She didn't answer so I answered myself, "They look like me. Can't you see that my children look like me?"

She nodded.

Then I asked her, "What similarity is there between you and I? You are not involved in the work of ministry. You are not a shepherd, you do nothing to help, and you do nothing in the church. You are a very nice person but not a daughter!"

She finally understood the point I was making. Just being around and being nice does not make you a son or a daughter. On that day, there were many children playing around after church, but only two of them were my sons. Being around doesn't make you a son. So what are the things that make you a son?

There are certain things that make you a son or a daughter, and that is what I want to share with you in this chapter.

Seven Signs of Sons and Daughters

1. A SON / DAUGHTER RESEMBLES HIS FATHER.

Jesus saith unto him, Have I been so long time with you, and yet hast thou not known me, Philip? HE THAT HATH SEEN ME HATH SEEN THE FATHER...

John 14:9

When you see my sons and daughters in the ministry, you will find that they have some resemblance to me. The similarities between sons and fathers are the telltale signs of the link between the fathers and the sons.

In the natural, my children look like me and even have my colour. Spiritually and in the ministry, there are many similarities between my sons in the Lord and myself. Jesus said, "He that has seen me has seen the Father."

The reason why I don't have to run around all the different churches preaching is because my sons and daughters are ministering powerfully. If you have seen the son, then you have seen the father.

A son is not a clone or a photocopy of the father. But he has very important and essential traits that he received from his father. Every son has his father's genes, blood type and DNA. There are some sons who take after their fathers so closely that they look very much like their fathers. On the other hand, there are sons who have very few similarities to their fathers even though they are real sons.

2. A SON / DAUGHTER IS FOREVER.

And the servant abideth not in the house for ever: but the Son abideth ever.

John 8:35

Real sons and daughters will always belong to the house. No matter what your natural child does, he always belongs to the house. He may have different beliefs but he belongs to the house. In his heart he knows where he belongs, he knows who brought him up and how he came to be what he is. A true son will scarcely rise up against his own father.

They went out from us, but they were not of us; for if they had been of us, they would no doubt have continued with us: but they went out, that they might be made manifest that they were not all of us.

1 John 2:19

3. **SONS AND DAUGHTERS BELIEVE IN THEIR FATHERS AND TRUST THEM FOR EVERYTHING.**

...Our Father which art in heaven, Hallowed be thy name. Thy kingdom come. Thy will be done in earth, as it is in heaven, Give us this day our daily bread.

And forgive us our debts, as we forgive our debtors. And lead us not into temptation, but deliver us from evil...

Matthew 6:9-13

Real sons are filled with lots of trust. Most work places are filled with untrusting people. The junior staff do not trust their manager. The managers do not trust their subordinates either.

But in a family, the children usually trust their father absolutely. I have never heard of children going on strikes or demonstrations against their parents.

The more we trust God, the more of His blessings we experience. Differences between children of the same family usually stem from different levels of trust they have for their father.

In the ministry, I notice the same thing. More of God's blessings and anointing flow through me to sons and daughters who are more trusting. Some sons and daughters are wary and suspicious. Others are more trusting and filled with faith. The trusting children always get more of their father's blessings. These differences come from the different extents to which they trust their fathers and what their fathers say.

If ye then, being evil, know how to give good gifts unto your children...

Luke 11:13

Jesus believed in His Father's ability. Jesus believed that His Father was powerful. Jesus understood the power of His Father. His very last words on the cross were to entrust Himself into His Father's care. "Father, into thine hands I commend my spirit."

With those words He plucked His soul out of the jaws of death and placed it into the hands of His Father.

And when Jesus had cried with a loud voice, he said, Father, into thy hands I commend my spirit: and having said thus, he gave up the ghost.

Luke 23:46

He believed in His Father and even when the terrors of death were closing in on Him, He knew who had the power to rescue Him. That is the power of a father, which Jesus respected. Is it not amazing that His very last words on earth shed such light on the son's belief in His Father? Stupendous!

4. A SON HONOURS HIS FATHER.

A son honoureth his father, and a servant his master: if then I be a father, where is mine honour...?

Malachi 1:6

Don't expect honour from servants or employees. You can only expect lip service and fake smiles from employees. You can expect honour from a real son. In the Old Testament, priests were essentially a group of children who ministered alongside their father.

One megachurch pastor said to me, "I have had many bad experiences by appointing pastors from other churches and Bible schools. Now I only have my own spiritual sons and daughters working with me in the ministry."

That is the way it should be! Your true sons and daughters will only bring you honour. Apart from a few prodigal sons, most sons and daughters bring honour and joy to their father.

God has often led me to honour people who have been fathers to me. I have tried to honour them in private and in public. I have honoured them with my words and with my substance.

True sons and daughters honour their father with their substance. It is a shame for your father or mother to struggle financially when you could help them. Do you want your parents to beg you for money? That is not honouring your father! That is humiliating him.

Even when your father and mother do not need anything, you must honour them with your substance because that is what the Bible teaches.

A son honoureth his father, and a servant his master: IF THEN I BE A FATHER, WHERE IS MINE HONOUR? and if I be a master, where is my fear? saith the LORD of hosts unto you, O priests, that despise my name. And ye say, Wherein have we despised thy name? Ye offer polluted bread upon mine altar; and ye say, Wherein have we polluted thee? In that ye say, The table of the LORD is contemptible. And if ye offer the blind for sacrifice, is it not evil? and if ye offer the lame and sick, is it not evil? offer it now unto thy governor; will he be pleased with thee, or accept thy person? saith the LORD of hosts.

Malachi 1:6-8

5. SONS OBEY THEIR FATHERS.

Children, obey your parents in the Lord: for this is right. Honour thy father and mother; (which is the

first commandment with promise ;) That it may be well with thee, and thou mayest live long on the earth.

Ephesians 6:1-3

Lots of rebellious people love to call themselves sons and daughters. They are no more sons and daughters than I am an astronaut. True sons obey their fathers! Do not try to exert authority over people who are not your true sons or daughters in the ministry. They will only disobey you because they are not your true sons and daughters. Your real sons and daughters will obey you.

When I sense that someone is not a son or daughter, I am very limited in what I tell the person to do. It is only true sons and daughters who obey.

6. SONS AND DAUGHTERS DO WHAT THEY SEE THEIR FATHERS DO.

...The Son can do nothing of himself, but what he seeth the Father do: for what things soever he doeth, these also doeth the Son likewise.

John 5:19b

A true son is looking out for what his father does. He is interested in what his father is doing and thinks that his father knows the right way. This is what Jesus did. He healed only those He saw His father healing and He preached only when He saw His father preaching.

Sons are rarely wiser than their fathers. Why didn't Jesus heal the whole multitude by the pool of Bethesda? He healed one man and left the rest untouched. It is like going into a hospital and healing only one person. It may not make sense to you but that is what the Father did. Jesus was content to do what He saw His Father doing.

I have sons and daughters in the ministry who flourish when they do what they see me doing. They preach what I preach and they teach what I teach. They see me healing the sick and they start to heal the sick. They do not do this because they are mindless clones; *they are simply good sons and good daughters!* Good sons are fast followers.

Of course, any human father (like me) is imperfect and his life will never be the perfect example of things to follow. Our ultimate example is Christ! But God gives fathers on this earth so that we have practical examples to follow.

7. SONS CARRY THE WORDS OF THEIR FATHERS.

A sign of a true son is that he carries the words of his father. He hears the words of his father often and he repeats them whenever he can. Sometimes you hear him repeating the words of his father in conversation and sometimes he preaches what his father has preached. As Jesus said, "He that hath seen me hath seen the Father."

People ask the sons, "How do you know all these things? Where did you get this wisdom from?"

But they are simply repeating the words of their fathers.

When I was a son to my father, Tender and the only son in the sight of my mother, then he taught me and said to me, "Let your heart hold fast my words; Keep my commandments and live;"

Proverbs 4:3-4 (NASB)

Chapter 7

Four Types of Sons

The nature of a son is revealed by his response to his father. Often, the good, the bad and the ugly come out when sons have to relate to fathers. There are four types of sons that the Scripture speaks about – the prodigal son, the elder son, the beloved son and the stubborn and rebellious son.

1.   CHARACTERISTICS OF A PRODIGAL SON

And he said, A certain man had two sons:

And the younger of them said to *his* father, Father, give me the portion of goods that falleth to *me*. And he divided unto them *his* living.

And not many days after the younger son gathered all together, and took his journey into a far country, and there wasted his substance with riotous living.

Luke 15:11-24

1. A prodigal son goes away from his father and his father's house

2. A prodigal son wants to be as far away from home as possible

3. A prodigal son wastes his life's opportunities

4. A prodigal son recognizes his mistakes in the midst of his life and returns to his father.

5. A prodigal son suffers the loss of many things because of his foolishness and his rebellious ways.

2.   CHARACTERISTICS OF AN ELDER SON

Now his elder son was in the field: and as he came and drew nigh to the house, he heard musick and dancing.

And he called one of the servants, and asked what these things meant.

And he said unto him, Thy brother is come; and thy father hath killed the fatted calf, because he hath received him safe and sound.

And he was angry, and would not go in: therefore came his father out, and intreated him.

And he answering said to *his* father, Lo, these many years do I serve thee, neither transgressed I at any time thy commandment: and yet thou never gavest me a kid, that I might make merry with my friends:

But as soon as this thy son was come, which hath devoured thy living with harlots, thou hast killed for him the fatted calf.

And he said unto him, Son, thou art ever with me, and all that I have is thine.

It was meet that we should make merry, and be glad: for this thy brother was dead, and is alive again; and was lost, and is found."

Luke 15:25-32

1. An elder son stays at home with the father.

2. An elder son never commits any major sins.

3. An elder son never strays off the straight and narrow path set for him by his parents.

4. An elder son does not live a life of pleasure and waste.

5. An elder son can develop a self-righteous and judgmental attitude towards people who stray away. Since he has never committed any of these sins himself he simply cannot understand why people should indulge in such foolishness. Pray that the father will be alive when the

prodigal son finally returns. If the prodigal son is left to the mercy of the elder brother it will not turn out well for him.

3.   CHARACTERISTICS OF A BELOVED SON

And Jesus, when he was baptized, went up straightway out of the water: and, lo, the heavens were opened unto him, and he saw the Spirit of God descending like a dove, and lighting upon him:

And lo a voice from heaven, saying, THIS IS MY BELOVED SON, in whom I am well pleased.

Matthew 3:13-17

And after six days Jesus taketh Peter, James, and John his brother, and bringeth them up into an high mountain apart,

And was transfigured before them: and his face did shine as the sun, and his raiment was white as the light.

And, behold, there appeared unto them Moses and Elias talking with him.

Then answered Peter, and said unto Jesus, Lord, it is good for us to be here: if thou wilt, let us make here three tabernacles; one for thee, and one for Moses, and one for Elias.

While he yet spake, behold, a bright cloud overshadowed them: and behold a voice out of the cloud, which said, THIS IS MY BELOVED SON, in whom I am well pleased; hear ye him.

Matthew 17:1-5

On two different occasions, the heavenly Father called Jesus Christ a beloved son; at the beginning of His ministry, (the baptism) and at the end of the ministry (the transfiguration). Jesus Christ was called the beloved son before He preached a single message or healed one sick person.

1. A beloved son is someone who submits to authority. Jesus was called a beloved son at the very beginning of His ministry when He accepted the humble conditions of His call.

2. A beloved son is a humble son. Jesus was a beloved son because He bowed down before John the Baptist even though He was the Son of God.

3. A beloved son is someone who is obedient to all instructions. A beloved son will obey an instruction whether it makes sense or not. A beloved son will obey an instruction whether it is easy or difficult. Jesus Christ was not just obedient to nice and easy instructions. He was obedient at every level. Beloved sons are obedient at all the different levels of obedience.

    Indeed, there are different levels of obedience but a beloved son will distinguish himself at every level. Each level of obedience leads to a different kind of blessing. Jesus Christ obeyed His father in coming to this earth to live amongst men and showing us God's love. Jesus Christ did the ultimate and obeyed His father even unto the death on the cross. Most Christians would struggle with instructions that would lead to their certain death. But not Jesus Christ! He was the quintessential "beloved son".

4. A STUBBORN AND REBELLIOUS SON

If a man have a stubborn and rebellious son, which will not obey the voice of his father, or the voice of his mother, and *that*, when they have chastened him, will not hearken unto them:

Then shall his father and his mother lay hold on him, and bring him out unto the elders of his city, and unto the gate of his place;

And they shall say unto the elders of his city, This our son is stubborn and rebellious, he will not obey our voice; he *is* a glutton, and a drunkard.

And all the men of his city shall stone him with stones, that he die: so shalt thou put evil away from among you; and all Israel shall hear, and fear.

Deuteronomy 21:18-21

Now you, son of man, listen to what I am speaking to you; do not be rebellious like that rebellious house. Open your mouth and eat what I am giving you.

Ezekiel 2:8 (NASB)

1. Stubborn and rebellious sons are resistant to instructions.

2. Stubborn and rebellious sons are opposed to the instructions.

3. Stubborn and rebellious sons dislike the person of their fathers.

4. Stubborn and rebellious sons dislike the methods of the father.

5. Stubborn and rebellious sons grow to dislike the ways of the father.

6. Stubborn and rebellious sons want a different profession from their father's.

7. Stubborn and rebellious sons want a different lifestyle from their father's.

8. Stubborn and rebellious sons want to dress, act and do everything differently from their father.

9. Stubborn and rebellious sons are angry at correction and need to be corrected for being angry at the correction.

Chapter 8

Dangerous Sons

There are some people who come out of your spiritual loins and are in reality your sons. Even though they are your sons, they can cause you great pain. As a leader, you must not be surprised if the people you bring up and train turn on you like wild tigers.

There are sons who carry the spirit of Absalom and such people are truly dangerous sons. *I call them dangerous because they are a part of you and yet they fight you.* They claim your heritage! They even look like you but the spirit of Absalom upon them changes everything.

How can you identify a son who will rise up against you to kill you? As usual, the Bible is the best guide for everything.

Twelve Signs of Dangerous Sons

1. A dangerous son is full of unforgiveness and bitterness.

And Absalom spake unto his brother Amnon neither good nor bad: for ABSALOM HATED AMNON, because he had forced his sister Tamar.

2 Samuel 13:22

And Jonadab, the son of Shimeah David's brother, answered and said, Let not my lord suppose that they have slain all the young men the king's sons; for Amnon only is dead: for by the appointment of Absalom THIS HATH BEEN DETERMINED FROM THE DAY THAT HE FORCED HIS SISTER TAMAR.

2 Samuel 13:32

Absalom was someone who did not forgive his brother for raping Tamar. He nursed the hatred in his heart for two years. He planned his revenge and eventually carried it out. This world

40

is a place of much offence. Many things will offend you in the church. Harbouring bitterness is the last thing that a minister should do.

I believe that the greatest temptation for a minister is the temptation to be unforgiving. This one sin will cut you away from God's love. In the Old Testament, there were some basic requirements for being a priest. A priest was not supposed to have unhealed wounds and sores. Unhealed wounds become infected and pollute the whole body.

A priest or a pastor was not allowed to carry around unhealed wounds. "No man with a crippled foot or hand or who is hunchbacked or dwarfed, or who has any eye defect, or who has *festering or running sores* or damaged testicles. No descendant of Aaron the priest who has any defect is to come near to present the offerings made to the LORD by fire. He has a defect; he must not come near to offer the food of his God. He may eat the most holy food of his God, as well as the holy food; yet because of his defect, *he must not go near the curtain or approach the altar*, and so desecrate my sanctuary. I am the LORD, who makes them holy" (Leviticus 21:18-23 NASB).

A true minister working in the vineyard will be wounded over and over. Jesus was wounded many times but he forgave. That is the example we must follow.

The commonest wounds experienced by pastors are the wounds inflicted by ungrateful and disloyal people. It is unbelievable how people forget the extent to which you have been a blessing to them. They turn on you. Many ministers cannot handle the ingratitude and disloyalty of people. The inability to handle ingratitude often becomes the turning point of their lives and ministries.

In the last interview of his life, Derek Prince was asked whether he had any regrets. Amazingly, he said that he regretted not forgiving the people who had hurt him as quickly as he should have.

To have become a minister is to have received extra mercy from God. This mercy is over and above the grace that is shown the average person. "It is God himself, in his mercy, who has given us this wonderful work [of telling his Good News to others], and so we never give up" (2 Corinthians 4:1, Living Bible). We are therefore expected to show mercy and forgiveness to those who offend us.

One day, I went for a walk with a pastor who had been betrayed by his assistant. As he spoke about this fellow, I noticed that he was trembling visibly. He could not believe what this disloyal associate had done to him. He had repaid all the goodness shown him with a slap in the face. I could virtually see the running sores and the open wounds on my brother. I felt sympathy for him because he was genuinely hurt. But I also worried for him because I knew it could be the end of his ministry.

You see, Absalom's unforgiveness was the beginning of his journey to desolation. Perhaps, Absalom would have been the King after David. But Amnon's wound turned Absalom into a hateful murderous beast.

Pastors are turned into bitter personalities by wounds that are inflicted on them from outside. Your reaction to something can kill you.

Asthma is a disease that reminds me of unforgiveness. Asthma is simply an overreaction to substances that irritate the lungs. In an attempt to keep out further irritants, the airways constrict and breathing becomes difficult. Death happens when this reaction goes too far.

Absalom overreacted to his brother's crime. As Absalom persisted on the road of unforgiveness, bitterness and revenge, he destroyed his life and ministry.

Somehow, God expects us to be even more forgiving. Perhaps the highest form of offence comes from spouses. Because marriage involves a physical and natural union, ministers are prone to multiple carnal wounds. Every minister must be resolute and unflinching in his or her resolve to be permanently married.

Never change your mind about your spouse. Do not allow your wounds and hurts to lead you into deception. All other options you may have on your mind will hurt you just as much as this marriage has. You do not have any options. Stay with what God has given you to the very end.

John Wesley was a good example of this. He had a difficult marriage but he stayed married to the same woman to the end of his life. Even though it was impossible to live with his wife, he remained married to her. He was separated from her but never divorced.

Marriage is for life. Good or bad, God expects you to forgive and walk in love. Watch out for people who do not forgive and forget.

2. *Dangerous sons attack their brothers.*

Now Absalom had commanded his servants, saying, Mark ye now when Amnon's heart is merry with wine, and when I say unto you, Smite Amnon; then kill him, fear not: have not I commanded you? be courageous and be valiant.

2 Samuel 13:28

Dangerous sons exhibit features, which are worrying to the experienced eye. Attacking and killing your own brother is a very bad sign and a cause for concern. You must recognize the danger signs of ministers who attack other colleagues.

Many pastors do not realize that most of their discussions centre on others and not on the Word of God. Constant analysis, criticism and mockery of fellow ministers are most common in the conversation of some pastors.

Many times, it is not even possible to share Scripture and revelations with one another. The discussions of jealous pastors seem to centre on criticizing what someone else is doing. I have noticed myself drawing away from the company of such ministers.

3. *Dangerous sons are not changed by years of hardship and difficulty.*

So Absalom dwelt two full years in Jerusalem, and saw not the king's face.

2 Samuel 14:28

Absalom suffered the hardship of living in exile for two years. One would have thought that he would undergo a change of heart. Watch out for pastors you have had to discipline and correct. The fact that they have been through punishment does not mean that they have repented. The spirit of unforgiveness and rebellion is simmering within.

I remember an employee whom we disciplined. He wrote an apology letter in which he said, "I was wrong and I apologize for what I did." After writing his letter, he was suspended from his work for some months. Somehow, after months of suspension, this dangerous son of mine rose up in rebellion against me. He attacked me and the church to which he had belonged.

At one point, he sent a message to me saying, "I will drive you out of this city." Perhaps, his intention was to spread enough bad stories about me until I was too embarrassed to stay in town.

Do these threats not sound familiar to you? Did Absalom not attempt to drive David out of Jerusalem? Actually, Absalom succeeded in driving David out of Jerusalem for some days.

The point is this: the spirit of Absalom is not corrected through punishment and even years of hard discipline. Do not be deceived into thinking that Absalom has changed just because he has been through a period of discipline, hardships or even poverty.

This explains why some people never apologize no matter what they go through. They may suffer so much but will not humble themselves and repent. Such people are simply Absalom reborn! Two years of exile and difficulty did not change the heart of Absalom. He became hardened and even more dangerous! A true "Absalom" is not humbled by his difficult experiences nor do they change him in any way!

4. *Dangerous sons feel that they cannot be dismissed.*

And Absalom answered Joab, Behold, I sent unto thee, saying, Come hither, that I may send thee to the king, to say, Wherefore am I come from Geshur? it had been good for me to have been there still: now therefore let me see the king's face; and if there be any iniquity in me, LET HIM KILL ME.

2 Samuel 14:32

Whenever a person feels indispensable he is a dangerous person to have around. Some people feel that they are untouchable and can never be dispensed with.

Absalom was someone who felt that he could not be sacked. He felt that he could not be transferred away.

We read about how Absalom told Joab that if King David found something wrong with him he should simply execute him.

Absalom felt that his father could not execute him. Absalom was sure that David could not punish or deal with him in a certain way.

These words of Absalom reveal the mindset of a dangerous person. "My father cannot sack me", "My father cannot discipline me", "My father cannot deal with me." In other words, I am untouchable and I know it!

Anyone who feels he is untouchable has developed the wrong attitude.

One day, I stood chatting with the most senior associate of a very large church. This man was seething because he had been transferred to another city.

The senior pastor had recognized the rebellion that was building up and had moved him quickly to another city.

But this fellow had thought that he was untouchable. He had also thought that it was an insult to be moved away from the church's headquarters.

We continued talking about his new position in a branch church.

He said, "I am a senior associate and I have worked here for many years. The concept of being transferred should not be applied to someone of my rank. I am above such things as being transferred."

He continued, "Even the word *'transfer'* should never have been applied to me..."

This fellow had thought that he was untouchable. He thought he was secure in his position forever. Unfortunately, as soon as you begin to think of yourself as indispensable, you are becoming proud and deceived. Just like Absalom, your delusions will lead to your destruction. Pride always comes before a fall.

Sometimes, people sense that they are special and loved and they take advantage of this special place that they have. That is also a mistake. There is always a Joab that will do the job that the father doesn't want to do.

There are circumstances that will eliminate a deluded and proud child from every good position he has. Try your luck and discover for yourself that no one is indispensable.

Dismiss Me if You Can

One time, a special son of mine behaved himself disrespectfully against the authority that was over him. There were several acts of insubordination. I tried to call him to reason with him but he would not even answer the telephone.

He would hear my voice on his answering machine and realize that I was desperately trying to get in touch with him. But he would not bother to answer.

Over a period of several weeks, we all tried to get in touch with him and to talk with him. He rudely ignored us until one day, his supervisor managed to get him on the phone. A short conversation ensued and I always remember a chilling message that this young man sent to all of us.

The overseer asked him, "Do you understand what you are doing?

Do you know how badly you are behaving?

Do you know how serious the situation is?

Do you understand the implications of what you are doing?"

He answered, "I do. I know what I am doing. I know the implications of everything."

His overseer said to him, "Then why are you doing what you are doing?"

He was insolently silent. Then he said, "Maybe you should sack me."

His overseer stuttered, "Did I hear you right? What did you say?"

He continued, "Any good organization would dismiss someone like me. It's up to you to dismiss me."

The conversation ended and the supervisor put down the phone in disbelief.

When the overseer told me about his conversation with this son of mine, I understood what was happening. You see this fellow felt that I could not sack him. He knew that he was special and he was pushing things to the limit. It is an "Absalom son" who knows that his father cannot kill him even when he deserves to die.

It was true that I could not easily dismiss him. Even after I received the invitation to sack this fellow, I decided to make one more manoeuvre to avoid dismissing him. I called his wife and told her to advise her husband to resign decently to prevent me from having to dismiss him.

As a father, I was making a move to prevent a son from destroying himself completely!

Absalom knew how much his father, David, loved him and he took advantage of it and said, "Let him kill me if he can."

Even when Joab executed Absalom, David lamented sorely over him.

And the king was much moved, and went up to the chamber over the gate, and wept: and as he went, thus he said, O my son Absalom, my son, my son Absalom! would God I had died for thee, O Absalom, my son, my son!

And it was told Joab, Behold, the king weepeth and mourneth for Absalom. And the victory that day was turned into mourning unto all the people: for the people heard say that day how the king was grieved for his son.

2 Samuel 18:33-19:2

Untouchable Wives

Wives who feel they cannot be divorced equally fall into this category. Some wives become mean and rebellious as they misuse the power of the marriage covenant, which opposes divorce. They feel they cannot be dismissed, divorced or replaced! They sense their husbands' commitment to the Word of God and exploit their untouchable status to the maximum.

They hide behind the curtain and manifest some of the ugliest behaviour possible on their powerless husbands.

A married minister is like a toothless bulldog that can bark but cannot bite. He can warn, rant and rave, but he cannot dismiss! And the wives know it!

Several ministers suffer silently at the hands of insane and wicked women who take full advantage of the "you can't divorce me" clause. For-For-Forgive!*

5.   *Dangerous sons think they can replace their fathers.*

... Absalom said moreover, Oh that I were made judge in the land, that every man which hath any suit or cause might come unto me, and I would do him justice!

2 Samuel 15:3-4

Absalom had a desire to take over and replace his father.

Absalom thought himself to be as good as his father David. This is the spirit of Absalom. "I can and will replace my father now." This is different from a son who wishes to emulate his father in the spirit of humility. This is a "takeover" and "replacement" spirit.

You Can Feel It

A bishop friend of mine could feel the spirit of Absalom all around him. He sensed these "dangerous sons with takeover spirits" hovering all around him in the ministry. These were hawks who felt their spiritual father was not relevant anymore.

He blurted out, "Some people are trying to retire me, but I cannot be retired!" He could sense that some people wanted him to leave the scene.

He continued, "What they don't know is that when I am gone, the 'thing' that was fighting me will begin to fight them."

Three Signs of the Replacement Spirit

Whenever such people start churches, they are unable to hide their desire to quickly become what their father is. An "Absalom" cannot hide the desire he has had for many years; the desire to take over and to replace his father.

Absalom said moreover, Oh that I were made judge in the land (2 Samuel 15:3-4).

This cry of the first Absalom is the same cry of all the present day "Absaloms". It is the unspoken wish of these dangerous sons!

It is interesting to watch these dangerous people operate. Their actions only reveal the bloodline from which they come. New and rebellious ministries founded by 'Absaloms' have certain features.

I want to show you three common features that I have noticed of churches and ministries that are started by dangerous sons with an Absalom spirit.

a. They love to locate their new church near the church that they broke away from.

These churches are often set up in the same area as their original church. A church I used to attend had a very popular associate pastor who broke away. This man published leaflets with damaging information against our senior pastor. One Sunday morning he distributed these leaflets as we all came to church. However, an army of ushers eventually rose up and threw him out of the front door.

This fellow was bewildered and stood outside the church building amazed that people could be loyal to someone he thought was unqualified. He felt he had enough damaging information to make the entire flock follow him. Instead he had been thrown out by loyal ushers.

Amazingly, he went a hundred meters down the same road and rented a hall thinking that the whole church would follow him there. Within a few months, his new church collapsed. "Absaloms" are sometimes very predictable. God does not bless the work of Absalom.

b. Another characteristic of these dangerous sons is that they use names similar to ones which their fathers use.

For instance, if the father's church was called "Losers International", Absalom's church is usually called "Defeat International". On the other hand, if the father's church is called,

"Heaven Chapel International," the Absalom's church is usually called something like "Paradise Chapel International".

Even within the church, they usually give similar names to things. For instance if the father's church choir was called "the Roses", Absalom's church choir would be called "the Lilies".

If cell groups were called "home fellowships", Absalom's cell groups would also be called "house fellowships" etc.

The reason for these similarities is that they are actually sons and a son has similar characteristics to his father. As I said, these "Absaloms" cannot hide their identity of being associated with their father.

In some cases, an "Absalom" would even keep the name of his father's ministry and fight over the name with him. I have seen amazing examples of breakaway churches which insisted on using the name of the original ministry, which they broke away from as their name. Amazing, isn't it?

c.   Dangerous sons have similar practices as their father.

Because Absalom learnt all that he knows from his father, he usually has similar practices in his church. For instance if the father's church had a midweek service on Thursday, Absalom would have his midweek service on Thursday as well. If his father's church had buses picking up members, Absalom usually does the same.

These are just a few similarities that prove that Absalom is truly a son, but a dangerous son indeed!

6.   *Dangerous sons criticize their fathers.*

And Absalom said unto him, See, thy matters are good and right; but there is no man deputed of the king to hear thee.

Absalom said moreover, Oh that I were made judge in the land, that every man which hath any suit or cause might come unto me, and I would do him justice!

2 Samuel 15:3-4

Absalom criticized his father's way of governing the country. Criticism is born of an evil spirit. There is simply nothing that justifies criticism. All of Scripture condemns this practice.

The Hog Vision

I once had a vision in which I found myself walking down a long lonely path in the midst of some mountains. Visibility was good and I could see for miles all around me. In the vision, I was chatting and walking with two other pastors.

At a point, I made a comment about a great man of God. My remark was not one of praise neither was it neutral: it was criticizing this man for something he had done.

As soon as the words came out of my mouth, I noticed a creature that I can best describe as a hog begin to walk in my direction. It was miles away and somewhere behind us but I noticed that it had begun to make its way towards me as soon as I made the remark. The creature seemed to have heard my critical remark. *Somehow, the complaint was the signal for it to start moving towards me.*

Initially, I thought the movement of that animal had nothing to do with me, but I felt uneasy and kept turning to see where it was.

To my dismay, it kept coming towards me. I realized that I was in danger and I turned round with my friends to face the creature as it walked rapidly and determinedly toward us. Finally, the creature caught up with us. To my surprise, the hog ignored my friends and leapt towards me, heading straight for my chest. I screamed as it entered my chest and then I woke up.

The Lord said to me, "Any time you criticize my servants, you attract evil spirits to your life."

These evil spirits bring sickness, disease and other plagues into your life. I realized that it was a very dangerous thing to speak against any of God's servants.

I was truly terrified by that vision.

Any spiritual person will be hesitant to speak against God's anointed, no matter the reason. Miriam felt she had a good reason to speak against Moses.

When she criticized him she was struck with leprosy and God asked her, "...wherefore then were ye not afraid to speak against my servant Moses?" (Numbers 12:8).

The Joshua Generation

The people that followed Moses never entered the Promised Land. They could not enter the Promised Land because of one thing: the spirit of complaining, murmuring, doubting and criticism.

So we see that they could not enter in because of unbelief.

Hebrews 3:19

How was this unbelief manifested? Unbelief is demonstrated by murmuring and complaining. The Israelites complained about everything. In the end, they did not enter the Promised Land. The Moses generation did not enter The Promised Land but the Joshua generation did.

The Joshua generation are the generation who put away complaining and grumbling.

The Promised Land will be inherited by the generation that stops murmuring. If you can stop all forms of murmuring and grumbling in your church, you will see God's promise for your ministry.

The Joshua generation knew all about the devastating effects of murmuring. The followers of Joshua promised to eliminate anyone who manifested even the faintest signs of grumbling.

And they answered Joshua, saying, All that thou commandest us we will do, and whithersoever thou sendest us, we will go.

According as we hearkened unto Moses in all things, so will we hearken unto thee: only the LORD thy God be with thee, as he was with Moses.

***Whosoever he be that doth rebel* against thy commandment, and will not hearken unto thy words in all that thou commandest him, he shall be put to death: only be strong and of a good courage.**

Joshua 1:16-18

Ham, the Dangerous Son

A son who grows up in your house and benefits from all that you have but still does not believe in you is a dangerous son. Such dangerous sons forget that they would not exist if their father had not been there. Such people forget that they would not be in the ministry if someone had not made it possible for them.

Ham found out that his father was drunk and decided to tell others about it. He scoffed at his own father! What Ham forgot was that if Noah had not built an ark, he would not even exist! If Ham had not been alive, how would he have been able to criticize his father Noah? That is why the curse of Ham is so severe. Do not criticize your father even if he is drunk. Rather pray for yourself that you will never have the same drinking problem.

The Cult Document

Once, I had some sons whom I raised and trained in the ministry. When I met them, they were ordinary Christians and very far from becoming ministers. I trained them and appointed them as pastors, set them in churches, encouraged them and protected them from things that destroy young ministers. There were times they made obvious mistakes that could have turned their congregations against them but I covered them and did not allow people to rebel against them.

On one occasion, when someone heard that I had been able to make a pastor out of one of them he exclaimed, "You are doing wonders!"

On another occasion, I defended this young pastor so much that I was accused of having ulterior motives. Sometimes, young ministers exhibit indefensible and unacceptable behaviour. However, as a father, it is my duty to protect my sons until they are able to stand on their own two feet. Eventually, these fellows departed from my ministry and no longer belonged to our church. Relating with them became an unpleasant experience for me because I realized that I was dealing with dangerous sons.

These were sons, but like Absalom, became an unpleasant experience to their father. I longed for them and thought about them often. I wished to have an input in their lives. However, it was not to be so.

My greatest shock came when I received a document from them that was a teaching about cults. In this document, the characteristics of cults were outlined. How to identify cults, and stay away from them!

Unfortunately, these two sons of mine had discovered through this teaching that Lighthouse Chapel, the church which had raised them, had some characteristics of a cult. They had shared these "truths" amongst themselves and were now sending me a copy to learn from it. I received my copy of the cult document. They wanted me to identify for myself the characteristics of my ministry that made what I was doing cult like.

Of course, I do not believe that I am the pastor of a cult. I pray for grace and mercy to be delivered from such a thing. However, I consider it a privilege to be derided for Christ.

These young men had forgotten, that the church in which they now saw the features of a cult, had ordained them into the ministry.

Is it not amazing that someone I raised would even think of me and my ministry as bearing a likeness to a cult! I don't even know of outsiders who could say such things. But such is life. Sons and daughters should be careful when making comments about someone who has been their father!

When Jesus cast out devils, someone made a comment about his using the spirit of Beelzebub. Jesus issued the most solemn warning ever:

Wherefore I say unto you, All manner of sin and blasphemy shall be forgiven unto men: but the blasphemy against the Holy Ghost shall not be forgiven unto men.

And whosoever speaketh a word against the Son of man, it shall be forgiven him: but whosoever speaketh against the Holy Ghost, it shall not be forgiven him, neither in this world, neither in the world to come.

Matthew 12:31-32

7. *Dangerous sons influence others against their fathers.*

And with Absalom went two hundred men out of Jerusalem, that were called; and they went in their simplicity, and they knew not any thing.

2 Samuel 15:11

False leaders thrive on the ignorance of their followers. Some people utterly dislike my book "Loyalty and Disloyalty". The reason they do not like it is that it exposes the disloyalty in them. Books on loyalty educate ordinary people in the church about the consequences of disloyalty. After such teachings, the ordinary church member easily identifies disloyal leaders. A grumbling, rebellious leader will stick out like a sore thumb and will not flourish where loyalty and disloyalty have been taught.

Once, I was invited to preach at a church. There were several pastors who sat on the front row of that church. I preached about loyalty and disloyalty. They all smiled with me after the service and gave neutral and pleasant comments about the sermon.

They said things like: "I was blessed", "good preaching" etc. Unfortunately, some of them actually hated the message. Later, one of them made a remark.

He said, "That book 'Loyalty and Disloyalty' is rubbish."

One of the pastors asked, "Does he not have anything else to preach about?"

Yet another said, "Is it only loyalty and disloyalty that he knows about?"

Not surprisingly, those who disliked the message were the disloyal pastors on the board. Within a few years, those disloyal pastors had left that church.

It is a clever strategy to discredit a book to your ignorant followers so that they never find out what is in it.

An Absalom thrives on the ignorance and naivety of the people. Watch out for people who campaign against their fathers, trying to make you turn against your own father.

8. *A dangerous son steals the hearts of the people from their father.*

And on this manner did Absalom to all Israel that came to the king for judgment: so ABSALOM STOLE THE HEARTS of the men of Israel.

2 Samuel 15:6

And there came a messenger to David, saying, THE HEARTS OF THE MEN OF ISRAEL ARE AFTER ABSALOM.

2 Samuel 15:13

Absalom needed to gain a following and he knew what to do. He had to win the hearts of the people. Unfortunately, Absalom had no right to the hearts of the people. That is why the Bible uses the phrase "he *stole* the hearts" of the people.

Dangerous sons want what does not belong to them. The most valuable thing a leader possesses is the heart of his followers. If their hearts are with you, then you are in control.

Leadership is all about winning the hearts of those you lead. David was a leader and he built the nation of Israel virtually from scratch. When he realized that the hearts of the people were with Absalom, he knew that he had to flee.

"Absaloms" are usually handsome or gifted individuals. Unfortunately, it is gifted, anointed and successful ministers who are tempted to become "Absaloms". Absalom had long, flowing hair and must have been attractive.

Every senior pastor must watch the "gifted" ones closely. It is a real temptation to become a dangerous son when you are gifted.

Mysteriously, the very gift that God gives can become a snare to you. As someone said, "Can you stand to be blessed?"

Can you carry an anointing? Can you carry an anointing for long?

Can you be gifted without become disloyal? Can you be a blessed son without becoming an Absalom?

Can you be rich without becoming proud?

Can you have access to the people without stealing their hearts?

Can anyone leave you in charge of his church without your taking over?

Can someone found a church and leave it in your care for a year without your stealing the hearts of the people?

Do not let your gift become your snare. Eventually Absalom was captured and killed because of his long, flowing hair. The blessing that God gave you will become what destroys you. How common this is. "And Absalom met the servants of David. And Absalom rode upon a mule, and the mule went under the thick boughs of a great oak, and his head caught hold of the oak, and he was taken up between the heaven and the earth; and the mule that was under him went away" (2 Samuel 18:9).

9. A dangerous son wants the pleasures and privileges of his father.

So they spread Absalom a tent upon the top of the house; and Absalom went in unto his father's concubines in the sight of all Israel

2 Samuel 16:22

The privileges of a father are special. It is important to respect the privilege that God has given to fathers. A son who desires the privileges of his father is truly an Absalom. Many ministers claim that God led them to begin their ministries. Actually, some of these men are "Absaloms" who want to enjoy the privileges of their father.

They are not content with what they have and see no reason why they should slave away and let someone else get all the big benefits.

If God has called you to start your own ministry, please make sure that you are not just another Absalom desiring the pleasure and privileges of senior pastors. The spirit of Gehazi and the spirit of Absalom merge at this point.

Gehazi desired more privileges while Absalom desired his father's concubines. "Absaloms" want more cars, houses and money. They want to be great and they want it quickly.

It is the fight for privileges that is often called the fight for "truth". In the name of fighting for the truth or fighting for God's will to be done, people are actually fighting for more privileges and pleasure spots. Forgive!

10. Dangerous sons have destructive tendencies.

Therefore Absalom sent for Joab, to have sent him to the king; but he would not come to him: and when he sent again the second time, he would not come. Therefore he said unto his servants, SEE, JOAB'S FIELD is near

mine, and he hath barley there; go and SET IT ON FIRE. And Absalom's servants set the field on fire.

2 Samuel 14:29-30

Absalom burnt down Joab's farm in order to get his attention. He would stop at nothing in order to have his way. Watch out for people who will stop at nothing to have their way.

They spend money recklessly and drive over people to have their way. You can see the ruthlessness in Absalom by this act of burning down Joab's farm. A ruthless person is a dangerous person. In their quest for power, they will do anything. They do not mind burning down the entire ministry or the reputation of their fathers in order to get their way.

11. *Dangerous sons are men of conspiracies, secret meetings and side discussions.*

And Absalom sent for Ahithophel the Gilonite, David's counseller, from his city, even from Giloh, while he offered sacrifices. AND THE CONSPIRACY WAS STRONG; for the people increased continually with Absalom.

2 Samuel 15:12

Absalom had several secret meetings with Ahithophel and other dissenters. These quiet meetings were necessary to develop a strong conspiracy.

There are people who love to whisper among themselves even in your presence. Whatever they say never seems to concern you! It is time to discern and to detect conspiracies among so-called loyal followers.

The success of any mission depends on the absolute loyalty of those with you. Fight for loyalty.

Keep your eyes open and notice people who have meetings after the official meeting. Watch out for people who have discussions on the side with private jokes which no one else understands. These are all signs that there is hidden information being kept from you.

12. *Dangerous sons lack the ability to induce loyalty in their followers.*

Dangerous sons are doomed to failure in ministry because they have been castrated of the power to induce loyalty. The testicles of loyalty have been removed and therefore there are no more seeds that can generate loyal followers.

After leading armies of people to kill your own father, how can you be established as a father?

The very foundation of loyalty and commitment is destroyed. The people you led have watched you destroy your own father. They have learnt by example about how to overthrow established and God-ordained leaders.

Removing Foundations

I remember visiting a pastor friend of mine who had just taken over a branch church of a certain denomination. He had painted over the original name of the church and renamed it.

He, together with the associates had conspired to rebel against the denominational headquarters and seize the entire church, including its assets, properties and members.

I challenged my friend, "How could you do something like this?"

Standing in the auditorium with him, I pointed out, "That is not your pulpit, and these are not your chairs."

I continued, "It is wrong to take over a church in this way."

But he was adamant, arguing that it was the will of God.

He explained, "Our General Overseer is backslidden and does not read the Bible any more. He just reads strange books like 'Attila the Hun'. "

"What is Attila the Hun?" I asked.

He answered, "I don't even know what 'Attila the Hun' is about because I refuse to read such things instead of the Bible."

Then he said, "Come, let me show you something."

He took me outside and there was a brand new, gleaming, black, German executive car. He said, "A man who heard of my takeover, bought this brand new car and sent it to me as a gift to encourage me. He did this to say 'thank you' to me for a good work done."

As we stood by this beautiful car, the pastor turned and looked into my face and said, "Can this be the devil? Is this not God at work? Would the devil give me such a beautiful and expensive car?"

To him, this surprise gift of a brand new car was a confirmation that he had done the right thing.

Then I asked, "How are you going to lead this new church?"

He said, "I am the pastor, but the others around me are going to have a share of the leadership. I don't want to run a one-man show as my former General Overseer did."

"I will be a different kind of leader," he continued.

As we parted company, I knew that this brother had removed the foundations for stability, leadership and loyalty. A few months later, his new associate pastors asked him to leave them. They levelled various accusations against him and showed him the door. He had no control over his associates because there was no foundation to that church. He was now powerless to control the raging storms of rebellion that he had unleashed.

Doomed to Reap a Harvest

Even if the people around you do not rebel, you are doomed to reap what you have sown. Galatians 6:7 will work against your good preaching, good principles, handsome appearance and clever strategies. It is just a matter of time. It may take ten years but the Scripture cannot be broken.

In the case of Absalom, he reaped what he had sown almost immediately. In his very first cabinet meeting, he was mistakenly led to choose a disloyal person as his chief counsellor.

God had determined to destroy Absalom and the Lord worked it out by making Absalom choose a disloyal person's advice.

Ahithophel had been part of the conspiracy for months and maybe even years. Hushai, the Archite, was actually a loyal friend of David who had been planted in Absalom's camp to mislead him. Absalom knew that the two wisest men whose advice his father had trusted were Hushai the Archite and Ahithophel the Gilonite.

Can you believe that Absalom chose to reject the counsel of his long-standing and loyal conspirator, Ahithophel, on that fateful night? This is the only thing that made Absalom lose the battle. He chose a disloyal person as his right-hand man.

Hushai: The Harvest of Absalom's Disloyalty

For they have sown the wind, and they shall REAP THE WHIRLWIND...

Hosea 8:7

If you are an "Absalom", God will make you choose evil because you have been evil to someone. You will unknowingly select wicked and unfaithful people. Liars and thieves will dance in circles around you. Your money will never be enough because the people that count and manage your money will steal from you constantly.

Treacherous women, more bitter than death, will be sent to destroy your life. Mercy! This is one of the punishments of God: "And I find more bitter than death the woman, whose heart is snares and nets, and her hands as bands: whoso pleaseth God shall escape from her; but the sinner shall be taken by her" (Ecclesiastes 7:26).

Wizards will be your accountants. You will unwittingly employ witches to assist you in the ministry. This is because when you were employed, you were a witch and a wizard to your employer. *Anytime there is a choice between a good person and a bad person, you will choose the bad person.* You will choose the wrong husband and the wrong wife. It will be a punishment and a snare to you for the rest of your days because you are not a loyal person.

If there is a good car and a defective car, you will always choose the defective one because when you were chosen you were evil to the one who chose you. If there is a good man and a bad man, you will always prefer the bad one. You will desire evil things and choose snares and traps for yourself because you were a snare to someone who loved you.

You will reap a hundredfold of your disloyalty and treachery! He that sows the wind will reap the whirlwind!

Many people do not realize that even the people you work with and lean on are gifts from God. *Absalom had the best options but he was doomed to choose the wrong thing.* Because he himself was a "wrong" child to his father.

I always pray that God will lead me to choose good people who will not harm me. Reaping and sowing are eternal principles of God's Word. Anyone who claims to be working for God must respect that law.

Chapter 9

Short Sighted Sons

And he said, A certain man had two sons:

And the younger of them said to his father, Father, give me the portion of goods that falleth to me. And he divided unto them his living.

And not many days after the younger son gathered all together, and took his journey into a far country . . .

Luke 15:11-13

There are sons who are obviously short sighted in their understanding of who a father is. In this chapter, I want to share what I believe are the characteristics of short sighted sons.

1. **A short sighted son is someone who sees his relationship with his father as a time-related contract rather than a lifelong experience.**

A short sighted son sees his relationship with his father as some short term encounter that he must go through. He relates with his father as though he were some lecturer who must be endured during a three-year course in the university. This sharply contrasts with permanent and continuous relationships that sons are supposed to have with their fathers.

A Father is a Tree

A long time ago, there was a huge mango tree. A little boy loved to come and play around it every day. He loved to climb the tree to the top, eat the mangoes, take a nap under the shadow... He loved the tree and the tree loved to play with him.

Time went by and the little boy grew up. He no longer played around the tree everyday. One day the boy came back to the tree looking sad. "Come play with me," the tree asked the boy.

"I am no longer a kid, I don't play around trees anymore," the boy replied."I want toys. I need money to buy them."

"Sorry, but I don't have money... but you can pick my mangoes and sell them. Then you will have money." The boy was so excited. He grabbed all the mangoes on the tree and left happily. The boy did not come back after he picked the mangoes. The tree was lonely and sad.

One day the boy returned and the tree was so excited. "Come and play with me" the tree said. "I don't have time to play. I have to work for my family. We need a house for shelter. Can you help me?" "Sorry but I don't have a house. But you can chop off my branches to build your house." So the boy cut all the branches off the tree and left happily. The tree was glad to see him happy but the boy did not come back to visit the tree.

The tree was lonely and sad. One hot summer day, the boy returned and the tree was so delighted. "Come and play with me!" the tree said.

But the boy said, "I am so sad and I am getting old. I want to go sailing to relax myself. Can you give me a boat? "

The kind old tree said, "You can use my trunk to build your boat. You can sail far away and be happy." So the boy cut the tree trunk to make a boat. He went sailing and did not show up again for a long time.

After many years the boy returned again to the same tree.

"Sorry, my boy, but I don't have anything for you anymore. No more mangoes for you..." the tree said.

"I don't have teeth to bite anyway," the boy replied.

The tree said, "I have no more trunk for you to climb on and play."

"I am too old for that now," the boy said.

Then the tree said, "I really can't give you anything.....the only thing left are my dying roots" the tree said with tears.

The boy replied, "I don't need much now, just a place to rest. I am tired after all these years."

The tree answered, "Old tree roots are the best place to lean and rest on." "Come, come sit down with me and rest." The boy sat down and the tree was glad and smiled with tears.

The tree is the father. When we were young, we loved to play with him. When we grew up, we left him only to come to him when we needed something or we were in trouble. Throughout life and through all the changing scenes of life fathers play a role to presumptuous children who think the fathers have nothing else to offer.

Presumptuous and short-sighted sons say, "My father's time is past. He is irrelevant to the times." But time, the weather, the elements and the realities of life will reveal to all of such people that a father is forever a father!

2. A short-sighted son sees his father as someone who is outmoded.

Many fathers are seen as food that has an expiry date or some item that has become outmoded or irrelevant. But a father never becomes irrelevant. Actually, fathers become more relevant as time goes by. If your mind is open and you have a humble spirit you will recognize that a father is not outmoded or irrelevant.

It is of the Lord's mercies that we are not consumed, because his compassions fail not. THEY ARE NEW EVERY MORNING: great is thy faithfulness.

Lamentations 3:22-23

Many of the blessings spoken in the Bible were given by fathers in the very last hours of their lives. Those words spoken by old departing fathers have affected generations of people. Isaac prophesied over his children in his last days. Obviously, he had not become irrelevant to the lives of his children. If he had been irrelevant what he said would not have come to pass.

3. A short-sighted son sees his relationship with his father in terms of certain "portions" he will get from his father.

Indeed, a short-sighted son has a limited understanding of the things he will get from his father. The prodigal son walked away from his father after asking for his "portion".

Some children see the relationship with their fathers in terms of money or items that they can receive. Because of this, they do not benefit from the true blessing of the father. For instance, some children look at their parents as someone to pay their school fees. Beyond school fees they do not expect or want anything else from their fathers. There are other children, like the boy in this story, who see their parents as people who will give them an inheritance. They are interested in the inheritance, seeing it as the only and worthwhile thing they can receive from their father. Some children even want their parents to die so they can acquire what their parents have.

Because of this short-sighted approach they lose out on the many intangible, but even more powerful aspects that a father brings to a son's life.

4. A short-sighted son does not see the invisible, non-tangible contributions that a father makes by his presence and influence.

There are many invisible and non-tangible things that a father brings into a child's life. How myopic can you be to think that your father's usefulness is limited to paying your school fees?

How truly myopic the prodigal son was when he thought his father's usefulness was limited to a portion of inheritance! What did he do with the portion of inheritance? Did he prosper with the portion of inheritance? Was he successful with a portion of inheritance? Did his life change even though he had that portion of inheritance?

Certainly not! He became poorer and lost everything even though he had gone away with a complete portion of inheritance.

Obviously there were certain unseen and perhaps intangible things that his father possessed that he had not yet received. Indeed he had a portion of inheritance but he had not received the wisdom and maturity that his father had to give. Without the wisdom, prudence and understanding of a father, money often amounts to nothing.

A father does not only pay school fees. A father provides stability, wisdom, direction, influence, guidance, security, safety and a host of other intangible blessings.

5.   **A short-sighted son is someone who quickly thinks he has received all he could ever receive from his father.**

A short-sighted son therefore disconnects from the umbilical cord long before he should have. He is quick to conclude that he has received everything the father has to offer.

There are many people who feel that they have received all the teachings that their father has. I have met many people who say within themselves, "I know what he teaches. I know what he has to say. I know what he does." You may ask, "How do I know?" It is the easiest thing in the world to perceive when you are with people who think they know you and they know all about you. Remember this is what the devil said to Jesus, "I know thee, who thou art." It is this line of thinking that evil spirits latch onto and inspire sons to abandon their fathers or leave the house unceremoniously.

I often notice pastors who think they know all about me. I smile to myself as they walk away with a portion they think they have received only to waste it and amount to nothing.

Sometimes a father gives a portion away but keeps some things which he intends to give at the very end. Isaac gave things to his sons at the very end of his life which he did not bother to give earlier. How immature and narrow-minded you show yourself to be when you think you have walked away with every bit of knowledge and wisdom your father has.

The Karate Master

There was once a master who was the karate champion of all the provinces. He was well versed in a hundred punches, kicking, knee and elbow strikes. He was also an expert in one hundred open hand techniques such as knife hands. He also knew a hundred grappling locks, restraints and throws.

Above all, he had ten vital point strikes which were his winning moves. This made up a total of three hundred and ten important karate moves.

He took a special liking to one of his pupils to whom he taught a total of three hundred and nine tricks. Somehow, he never got around to teaching him the last vital move.

As the months went by the pupil became so good at karate that he boasted that he could beat everyone including his master. Indeed, he said it was only out of respect for his age and gratitude for what he had been taught that he would not humiliate his master. In the process of time the master heard about his pupil's bragging and decided to teach his disciple a lesson. He offered himself for a match with his pupil and crowds gathered to watch the only young man who could defeat the master.

When the gong sounded the disciple rushed at his master only to be confronted with the unfamiliar three hundred and tenth karate strike. The master lifted his former pupil above his head and flung him headlong to the ground amidst loud cheers from the audience.

Later, when he was asked how he was able to defeat such a strong young man the master confessed that he had reserved the three hundred and tenth secret technique for himself in case of such an event.

Indeed, there are many sons and disciples who think they have learnt everything that there is to learn, only to discover to their dismay that there were many more things that they could have learnt.

Chapter 10

Three Rewards for Honouring Fathers

Children, obey your parents in the Lord: for this is right. Honour thy father and mother; which is the first commandment with promise; THAT IT MAY BE WELL WITH THEE, AND THOU MAYEST LIVE LONG ON THE EARTH.

Ephesians 6:1-3

1. **The first reward for honouring fathers: That it may be well with you**

    1. When it is well with you, you will be successful.

    2. When it is well with you, you will overcome.

    3. When it is well with you, you will thrive.

    4. When it is well with you, you will flower.

    5. When it is well with you, you will multiply.

    6. When it is well with you, you will recover.

    7. When it is well with you, you will hit it big.

    8. When it is well with you, you will prosper.

    9. When it is well with you, you will develop.

    10. When it is well with you, you will increase.

    11. When it is well with you, you will win.

    12. When it is well with you, you will get ahead.

    13. When it is well with you, you will do well.

14. When it is well with you, you will bear fruit.

15. When it is well with you, you will expand.

One of the highest blessings is that it may be well with you. Who would not like it to be well with him? However, it will never be well with you if you are disobedient to your father!

The greatest blessing for sons is hidden in their obedience to their fathers. There is something I have noticed in large families with many children.

The sons or daughters who are very obedient to their parents turn out differently from those who are rebellious, independent and resistant. It is a pattern you will discover for yourself.

One pastor told me how she had noticed this phenomenon. She described how some of her father's children had constantly resisted their father's advice. "It is not easy for them today", she said. "Marriage is not easy. And financially, it is very difficult for them."

She continued, "I can see a clear difference between those of us who obeyed and those who rebelled."

The Difference Is Clear

Another pastor said to me, "I have a big family with many brothers and sisters but the difference is clear."

He described how his father was cared for by one of his daughters.

He said to me, "This sister of mine cared for my father all the time. She did what he wanted and he was always pleased with her."

"In fact", he continued, *"my father died in her arms. She was nursing him when he died. Even my mother was not around when he died but she was there."*

Today, her life is very different from some of her brothers and sisters. He began to describe horrific conditions of the cancer and poverty which had struck some of his other brothers and sisters. He mused, "There is certainly a difference between children who love and honour their parents and those who don't."

One day, a father went shopping with his two sons. As they walked through the department store buying clothes, the father suggested to his sons, "Take this pair of trousers, it will suit you, it is nice." But there was a clear difference in the response of the sons to their father's suggestions.

One of them constantly had a different opinion. He didn't like what his father liked. He always wanted something different. He even became grumpy and angry because he couldn't have some things.

However, the reaction of the other son was very different. He would say, "Whatever you choose for me is okay. I like what you like for me. *I want what you want for me*."

You see, these two attitudes can grow up and result in two different outcomes. The highest kind of blessing is that it may be well with you. It will be well with daughters who trust and obey their fathers! It will be well with sons who trust and obey their fathers. This principle applies to all kinds of fathers whether natural or spiritual.

Become a son who wants what his father wants for him. Become a son who likes what his father likes. Christianity is based on this principle: the principle of submitting your will to the will of your father. The principle of *accepting the father's will* instead of your own will.

Do not be self-willed. Be subject to your father's will. It is safer and easier to say, "Father, into thine hands do I commit my life." Let's follow Jesus; He is the best example for us all.

2. The second reward for honouring fathers: That you may live long

1. When you honour your father you will overcome diseases that shorten life.

2. When you honour your father you will survive many crises.

3. When you honour your father you will continue in spite of danger.

4. When you honour your father you will endure many difficulties.

5. When you honour your father you will last a long time.

6. When you honour your father you will stay alive when people predict your death.

7. When you honour your father you will live to tell the tale.

8. When you honour your father you will be able to persist in the ministry.

9. When you honour your father you will prolong your life.

10. When you honour your father you will stay afloat.

11. When you honour your father you will make a comeback.

12. When you honour your father you will outlast others.

13. When you honour your father you will outlive others.

14. When you honour your father you will outwear others.

15. When you honour your father you will pull through.

16. When you honour your father you will tough it out.

17. When you honour your father you will come through.

18. When you honour your father you will go all the way.

19. When you honour your father you will 'never say die'.

20. When you honour your father you will be timeless.

One of the sure ways to shorten your life is to dishonour fathers and mothers. Look around carefully and you will find this to be practically true.

In the ministry, your longevity is also determined by your relationship with your fathers. Longevity speaks of how long you last in the ministry. You will always meet people ahead of you. It is important to honour these people as fathers. Even when you have a different ministry, you must respect the fathers for who they are.

Two examples of long-lasting ministries are those of Jesus and David. Jesus' ministry has spanned thousands of years and is getting stronger. The ministry of King David is still being felt through the Psalms he wrote and the life he led. If you want to survive and persist through the years, learn this principle now!

3.   **The third reward for honouring fathers: Receiving an inheritance**

> **The eyes of your understanding being enlightened; that ye may know what is the hope of his calling, and what the riches of the glory of his inheritance in the saints**
>
> **Ephesians 1:18**

There is something known as a spiritual inheritance. A "spiritual inheritance" is something that passes from fathers to sons. Only when you receive your man of God as a *father* do you receive the benefit of an inheritance. An inheritance will only flow from the *fathers* to their *sons and daughters*.

You will notice from the story of Elisha that he had an earthly father called Shaphat.

> **...Here is Elisha the son of Shaphat...**
>
> **2 Kings 3:11**

However, at the time Elijah was being taken away, Elisha referred to Elijah as his father. He did this effortlessly and naturally.

> **And Elisha saw it, and he cried, My father, my father...**
>
> **2 Kings 2:12**

Why is it important to receive your man of God as a father? *It is because fathers leave behind an inheritance for their children.* People usually do not leave an inheritance for servants, employees, friends and colleagues. The inheritance is meant for the children!

A person with an inheritance is very different from someone without one. A person with a father receives guidance and direction for his life. A fatherless person has a life full of struggles.

I never worked while I was in the university. My father provided for me fully until I became a doctor. The money he gave me each month as a student was more than my salary when I became a doctor. My father bought me a brand-new car when I was in the fifth year of medical school. I was really blessed to have a good father looking after me. *My life as a student was "struggle-free" because I had a father!* However, the same cannot be said for many people.

I have met countless people who did not receive guidance for their lives. They threw away their talents and became non-entities because there was no father to guide them. I know many people who do not even know their fathers.

The situation is even worse for orphans! Struggles abound for orphans. The future of an orphan is very uncertain. It is the same in ministry. When you have no one to influence you in the right way, your ministry is full of struggles. Although I have had different fathers in ministry, there were times I was fatherless as far as developing into a pastor was concerned.

I have had fathers in ministry from afar. I have gone through various struggles because I did not receive support from nearby fathers. Many of the struggles and frustrations I experienced in ministry were because I had no one to help me.

In fact, people who should have been fathers to me when I was beginning my church were more of outright enemies. They opposed my cause and fought against me.

Inheritance flows naturally from a father to his children. In the ministry, spiritual inheritance flows naturally from the fathers to the sons. When my father died, his Will was read in Court. He left his properties to his children. Although he had many employees and friends he didn't will anything to them — everything went to his children. Dear friend, that is the reality of life. The inheritance always goes to children and not to colleagues and friends.

There is something known as a spiritual inheritance. This spiritual inheritance of anointing and gifts passes naturally from fathers to sons. It does not pass from father to equals, colleagues and friends. It does not even pass from father to servants. It passes from *fathers to sons*.

Hello "Boss"

I used to have a junior pastor who preferred to call me "boss". I always felt uneasy when he called me "boss", but I didn't know why. You see, when someone calls you "boss", it means that he sees himself more as a hired hand. A few years later this pastor departed under unpleasant circumstances. Then I realized why I had felt uneasy. A servant or an employee does not stay around forever. He's only there for a while and will leave when it suits him.

And the servant abideth not in the house for ever: but the Son abideth ever.

John 8:35

If you have a relationship with a man of God, which becomes a father-son relationship, you can expect a spiritual inheritance of anointing to flow effortlessly from him to you.

Chapter 11

Seven Supernatural Powers of a Father

1. The father's supernatural power to be a stepping stone

And Simeon blessed them, and said unto Mary his mother, Behold, THIS *CHILD* IS SET FOR THE FALL AND RISING AGAIN OF MANY in Israel; and for a sign which shall be spoken against;

Luke 2:34

A father, by his very existence, causes his children to go higher. The Scripture above shows us how the presence of Christ caused the rise and the fall of many different people. A father is supernaturally placed to cause the elevation and promotion of his sons.

Fathers do not have to speak a blessing in order to be a blessing to their sons. All they have to do is to exist, and their children will be blessed. Most fathers do not say anything special to their children. Just the existence of the father causes the child to be blessed.

That is why people feel sorry for children whose father is dead. What they are concerned about is not the absence of spoken blessings or curses. The going away of the father's presence is the problem. His absence will have an effect of untold dimensions on the children.

2. The father's supernatural power to be a stumbling block

A father does not have to speak a curse in order to cause problems for his sons. A father's existence can cause the fall of his son. Because fathers are not perfect they are easy to criticize and dishonour. Fathers often look strange and outdated to sons.

Now when John had heard in the prison the works of Christ, he sent two of his disciples, And said unto him, Art thou he that should come, or do we look for another?

Jesus answered and said unto them, Go and shew John again those things which ye do hear and see:

The blind receive their sight, and the lame walk, the lepers are cleansed, and the deaf hear, the dead are raised up, and the poor have the gospel preached to them.

And BLESSED IS HE, WHOSOEVER SHALL NOT BE OFFENDED IN ME.

Matthew 11:2-6

Jesus said that people who were not offended by Him were blessed. Jesus knew that even though He was doing good works there would be people who would be offended by Him. It does not take much to offend people! People are offended by almost everything! Temperamental sons can easily get on the wrong side of the road and walk in bitterness towards a father. Sons who fall into the trap of dishonouring fathers earn themselves a solid biblical curse!

But how and when will this curse be spoken? What you must realise is that fathers need not speak any curses themselves. Don't worry about whether the father has spoken a curse or not. The Word of God has numerous written curses for sons who dishonour fathers in one way or the other. In this way, fathers who never speak a curse actually cause curses to come upon children.

3. The Father's Supernatural Power to Speak a Curse

Fathers have the power to bless and to curse. They occupy a seat of authority given by the Lord. There is tremendous power released when a father speaks a blessing over a son.

There are three groups of people on earth that have been given divine authority. In the family setting, the father has been given authority. In the nation, the government has been given authority, and in the church, the pastor is the authority figure.

Everyone must submit himself to the governing authorities, for there is no authority except that which God has established. The authorities that exist have been established by God.

Consequently, he who rebels against the authority is rebelling against what God has instituted, and those who do so will bring judgment on themselves.

Romans 13:1-2 (New International Version)

Your relationship with any of these authorities is vital for your existence on this earth. Any kind of father assigned to you by God is an authority in your life.

If the spirit of the ruler rise up against thee, leave not thy place; for yielding pacifieth great offences.

Ecclesiastes 10:4

One day, I was in a lobby having a chat with some pastors. I overheard another pastor describing his woes. His child was in a coma and he had spent all his money trying to save the life of his child. He was now broke and desperate. In his own words, he described what he felt had led to his predicament.

He had had a disagreement with an authority in his life and as he walked away from this authority, the father declared, "My covering has been removed from you."

"That was the beginning of all my troubles," he said.

You see, spiritual people understand spiritual principles. Strive to get the blessings rather than the curses of an authority figure.

Deadly Curses

The curse of a father is deadly! A father is an authority figure and his words have heavenly backing. Fatherhood is actually a spiritual position. Words coming from this position contain power and must not be taken lightly. The Bible is full of examples of curses and blessings.

The Curse of Ham

Noah was a type of Adam in the sense that he was the only man on earth and had to repopulate the earth with his children. Noah built the ark and escaped the floods. He and his family were the only people alive on the earth after the flood.

However, one day something happened that changed the course of history even more than the flood itself. This was the day Noah had too much to drink and lay naked in his tent. One of his sons, Ham, the dark-skinned fellow, exposed his father's nakedness and told others about it. However, the other two children covered their father's nakedness.

When Noah woke up, he delivered one of the most frightening rebukes of all time. He pronounced "the curse of the servant of servants" on his son. This pronouncement, directed at the dark-skinned son, has had an effect that is felt up till today.

All over the world, black people are treated as second-rate beings. Billions of dollars are spent to fight wars and free oppressed people in Iraq. But there is no motivation to help the slaughtered sons and daughters of Liberia and Sierra Leone.

A *twenty-million dollar* reward was offered for information leading to the capture of Saddam Hussein or his two sons.

But in Africa, only *twenty-thousand dollars* was offered to capture the African terrorist Mohammed Farrah Aided.

Black people all over the world are suffering from the frightening rebuke and curse of Noah. The continent occupied by black people is generally seen as a sub-standard place occupied by inferior people. Yet, it is the continent with the richest mineral resources. Some of the largest gold mines in the world can be found in African countries like Tanzania, Ghana and South Africa.

Even within each continent, the parts occupied by black people are seen as second-rate zones. Whether it is black people in North or South America, black people in Australia or black people in Europe, the picture is the same. It is the picture of the servant or the servant of servants.

How could such a unique pattern be established throughout the world? It has been shown that black people are as intelligent as white people. The American space shuttle that crashed had a black astronaut on board. Black people have achieved equally great heights in education as white people.

The President of the United States of America, the best golfer, the richest woman, the best basketball player, the fastest male and female athletes, the best and richest boxers in the world are all black people. The king of pop music and the best-selling Christian musician ever, are both black men.

Still, the curse and the rebuke continue to daunt the black man. The words spoken by the father against his son, echo through the centuries, producing an unmistakable pattern of servanthood.

Manage Your Relationship with Fathers

One of the wisest things on earth is to carefully manage your relationship with fathers.

When young people fall in love, they often forget the importance of honouring and obeying their parents. Some time ago, I did not recognize this principle to its fullest. But I appreciated it when two young ladies died in the midst of their years after marrying against their parents' wishes.

One husband described how his wife's family was totally against his marriage. But he insisted and went on against his parents' wishes. The young lady developed a strange form of paralysis. When she died, she left behind little children for her husband to take care of.

Marrying against a Father's Wishes

I remember sitting on the hospital bed of a dying twenty-five year old girl. Her father was against her getting married but she had gone ahead and married without her father's knowledge.

Because of my medical experience, I know when somebody is dying. I can tell by just looking at their faces. I was petrified as I sat on her bed. She put her hand on my knee and said to me, "Bishop, are you afraid?" Unfortunately, I lied. I was scared out of my wits. But I said I was not afraid.

Then she told me, "Don't be afraid, I am not going to die." But I knew she was dying. I put my hand on her head and palpated several bumps, which seemed to be metastatic cancerous lesions to her skull. She had a rare and terrible cancer, which had spread all over. The disease was so strange that it was only diagnosed fully at her post-mortem.

She died in a horrible and frightening way, which I have never forgotten. Throughout the ordeal, my mind was constantly on how she had gone against her father's wishes. Truly, the curse of the father must be avoided at all costs. Obey, flow in peace towards the fathers that God gives to you. They are given for your good.

> Everyone must submit himself to the governing authorities, for there is no authority except that which God has established. The authorities that exist have been established by God.
>
> Consequently, he who rebels against the authority is rebelling against what God has instituted, and those who do so will bring judgment on themselves. For rulers hold no terror for those who do right, but for those who do wrong. Do you want to be free from fear of the one in authority? Then do what is right and he will commend you.
>
> Romans 13:1-3 (NIV)

The eye that mocketh at his father, and despiseth to obey his mother, the ravens of the valley shall pick it out, and the young eagles shall eat it.

Proverbs 30:17

4.   The father's supernatural power to speak a blessing

And it came to pass, that when Isaac was old, and his eyes were dim, so that he could not see... And his father Isaac said unto him (Jacob)... Therefore God give thee of the dew of heaven, and the fatness of the earth, and plenty of corn and wine: Let people serve thee, and nations bow down to thee: be lord over thy brethren, and let thy mother's sons bow down to thee: cursed be every one that curseth thee, and blessed be he that blesseth thee.

Genesis 27:1,26,28,29

And it came to pass after these things, that one told Joseph, Behold, thy father is sick...And he blessed them that day, saying, In thee shall Israel bless...

Genesis 48:1, 20

Unfortunately, natural men have mistaken physical weakness for spiritual weakness. They presume that old age, sickness and problems reduce a person's spiritual authority. That is one of the highest kinds of deceptions.

Isaac was an *old blind man.* He could no longer see the difference between his two sons, Jacob and Esau. Isaac was deceived by Jacob and in his deception, he spoke a blessing over Jacob and it came to pass.

And he said, Art thou my very son Esau? And he {Jacob} and said, I am. And he came near, and kissed him...and blessed him, and said, See...the LORD hath blessed; Therefore God give thee of the dew of heaven, and the fatness of the earth, and plenty of corn and wine: Let people serve thee, and nations bow down to thee: be lord over thy brethren, and let thy mother's sons bow down to

84

thee: cursed be every one that curseth thee, and blessed be he that blesseth thee.

Genesis 27:24, 27-29

Do not be misled by the blindness and weakness of your father. He is still a father and that is the main lesson of this chapter. If a blind father can speak a blessing that comes to pass, then we must fear the words of fathers.

You often hear people speaking against their fathers. They describe them as irresponsible men who didn't look after them. They don't want to have anything to do with their fathers. Sometimes in our youthful healthy state, fathers are seen as short-sighted, eccentric men, whose contribution is irrelevant.

Unfortunately, some young people take up the hurts of their mothers and champion the fight against their fathers. This is a terrible mistake for which they pay a high price. Some pay the price of barrenness; some pay the price of death. Yes, he may be blind, irresponsible, and deceived, but he is still a father.

Many men of God in their latter years look battle-weary and drained. They are often presented as fallen heroes, men of the past, forgotten ghosts! No one wants to have anything to do with them. But it is these "blind and deceived people", who brought you forth and gave you the heritage you have today.

When Ham exposed the nakedness of his drunken father, he forgot one thing. He forgot that if his father hadn't built the ark, he would have drowned. He would have drowned with the rest of the world. His body would have been eaten by sharks, barracudas, herrings, tuna, piranha and red fishes!

What he did not know was that through his father's single act of faith, the whole world was saved. What he did not know was that God had recorded that act of faith and imputed it to him as righteousness. *Ham was disgracing someone that God had honoured.*

May we never be part of the team that dishonours the fathers that God has honoured!

5. The father's supernatural power to cover his children

He shall cover thee with his feathers, and under his wings shalt thou trust: his truth *shall be thy* shield and buckler.

Psalms 91:4

Jesus and His Father

Jesus understood the power of His father. His very last words on the cross were to entrust Himself into His Father's care. "*Father*, into thine hands I commend my spirit." With those words He plucked His soul out of the jaws of death and placed it into the hands of His Father.

He trusted His Father and even when the terrors of death were closing in on Him, He knew who had the power to rescue Him. That is the power of a father, which Jesus respected. Is it not amazing that His very last words on earth shed such light on the power of a father?

I will meet them as a bear *that is* bereaved *of her whelps*, and will rend the caul of their heart, and there will I devour them like a lion: the wild beast shall tear them.

Hosea 13:8

Parents are supernaturally empowered to protect their children. Every single animal species has been known to risk their lives to protect their young. The supernatural strength to fight every kind of enemy that threatens a child is a God-given ability. When God gives you a father, he will meet your enemies in a gate like a bear robbed of her whelps.

There is no one who is as divinely inspired to lay down his life for your protection other than a father. Fathers are given supernatural power to fight for the lives of their children.

6. The father's supernatural power to know what is right

Children, obey your parents in the Lord: for this is right.

Ephesians 6:1

Many times we seek to know what to do. Should I go *this way* or *that way*? What is *right* and what is *wrong*? Often parents know what is the best thing to do for their children. Most parents have the best interests of their children at heart. This is why what they say is often right.

The Scripture above says clearly that obeying parents is the right thing to do. From now on, when you want to know what the right thing is, think of what instructions you have been given by your parents.

Spiritual fathers have the same supernatural power to know what is right for their spiritual children. Many times what the father says is the right thing. How much easier can things get? Obeying fathers is the right thing to do!

7. The father's supernatural power to feed his children

When a child is born the mother is supernaturally empowered to produce milk that will be the food of the child. Before the mother becomes pregnant her breasts are simply mounds of fat. They are completely dry of milk. It is amazing how milk-forming glands develop just because a child is expected.

Similarly, God gives supernatural powers to His fathers and mothers to provide food for His children. A pastor who is anointed by God is supernaturally empowered to father his flock and provide all the spiritual food they need.

It is a marvel that a man can stand before the same congregation and preach to them for thirty years. You would wonder where the pastor gets his messages from. You would wonder whether the people would not be tired of him. And yet, most of the congregation become so attached to this shepherd that they do not seem to understand other preachers.

God gives supernatural ability to the father of the children to feed them.

Chapter 12

How Fathers Cause the Rise and the Fall of Many

... this child is set for the fall and rising again of many ...

Luke 2:34

This is an ancient prophecy about Jesus Christ, our Lord and King, and the effect that He would have on many people. Through Him many would rise and through Him many would fall. Jesus Christ is our shepherd, our Lord, our Saviour and our King. Amazingly, He would cause some people to fall and some people to rise. Jesus did not only caused people to do well but caused the fall and destruction of those who responded wrongly to Him.

Fathers also affect their sons' in two ways. Fathers may bless their children causing them to rise, or they may curse them causing them to fall.

The father and all that he represents also provoke certain reactions and responses from children. These reactions vary from child to child and cause either a rise or fall of that child.

When a child responds wrongly to a father, he incurs the debilitating effect of ancient curses against such children. Truly, you do not have to live long to discover what becomes of people who do not respond properly to fathers.

This book seeks to reveal both the blessings and the dangers that are present in relationships with fathers. Many people do not recognize the power and authority that fathers carry. A father is someone who brings you into existence. That is what gives him such authority and power over your life.

Below is a list of Scriptures that show how sons either rose or fell through their relationships with fathers.

1.   **Fathers cause the earth to be smitten with a curse when their hearts are turned away from their sons.**

   And he shall turn the heart of the fathers to the children, and the heart of the children to their fathers, lest I come and smite the earth with a curse."

Malachi 4:6

2.   **Fathers cause the earth to be smitten with a curse when their sons' hearts are turned away from their father.**

   And he shall turn the heart of the fathers to the children, and the heart of the children to their fathers, lest I come and smite the earth with a curse."

Malachi 4:6

3.   **Noah caused the rise of his son Shem by blessing him specially.**

   Then Noah said, "May Shem be blessed by the LORD my God; and may Canaan be his servant.

Genesis 9:26 (NLT)

4.   **Noah caused the rise of his son Japheth by predicting his enlargement.**

   God shall enlarge Japheth, and he shall dwell in the tents of Shem; and Canaan shall be his servant.

Genesis 9:27

5.   **Isaac caused the rise of his son Jacob by blessing everyone that blessed him and cursing everyone that cursed him.**

   Therefore God give thee of the dew of heaven, and the fatness of the earth, and plenty of corn and wine:

   Let people serve thee, and nations bow down to thee: be lord over thy brethren, and let thy mother's sons bow down to thee: cursed be every one that curseth thee, and blessed be he that blesseth thee."

Genesis 27:28-29

And Isaac called Jacob, and blessed him ... And God Almighty bless thee, and make thee fruitful, and multiply thee, that thou mayest be a multitude of people; And give thee the blessing of Abraham, to thee, and to thy seed with thee; that thou mayest inherit the land wherein thou art a stranger, which God gave unto Abraham."

Genesis 28:1-4

6. **Jacob caused the rise of his son Judah by speaking many blessings over his life.**

Judah, thou *art he* whom thy brethren shall praise: thy hand *shall be* in the neck of thine enemies; thy father's children shall bow down before thee. Judah *is* a lion's whelp: from the prey, my son, thou art gone up: he stooped down, he couched as a lion, and as an old lion; who shall rouse him up?

The sceptre shall not depart from Judah, nor a lawgiver from between his feet, until Shiloh come; and unto him *shall* the gathering of the people *be*. Binding his foal unto the vine, and his ass's colt unto the choice vine; he washed his garments in wine, and his clothes in the blood of grapes: His eyes *shall be* red with wine, and his teeth white with milk.

Genesis 49:8-12

7. **Jacob caused the rise of his son Zebulun by extending his borders.**

Zebulun will settle on the shores of the sea and will be a harbor for ships; his borders will extend to Sidon.

Genesis 49:13 (NLT)

8. **Jacob caused the rise of his son Gad by prophesying that he would overcome at the end.**

Gad, a troop shall overcome him: but he shall overcome at the last.

Genesis 49:19

9. **Jacob caused the rise of his son Asher by speaking blessings over him.**

    Out of Asher his bread *shall be* fat, and he shall yield royal dainties.

    Genesis 49:20

10. **Jacob caused the rise of his son Joseph by blessing him and by predicting that God would be with him and by giving him one portion above his brethren.**

    And Israel said unto Joseph, Behold, I die: but God shall be with you, and bring you again unto the land of your fathers.

    Moreover I have given to thee one portion above thy brethren, which I took out of the hand of the Amorite with my sword and with my bow.

    Genesis 48:21-22

    Even by the God of thy father, who shall help thee; and by the Almighty, who shall bless thee with blessings of heaven above, blessings of the deep that lieth under, blessings of the breasts, and of the womb:

    The blessings of thy father have prevailed above the blessings of my progenitors unto the utmost bound of the everlasting hills: they shall be on the head of Joseph, and on the crown of the head of him that was separate from his brethren."

    Genesis 49:25-26

11. **Jacob caused the rise of his son Benjamin by declaring that he would divide the spoil.**

    Benjamin shall ravin as a wolf: in the morning he shall devour the prey, and at night he shall divide the spoil.

    Genesis 49:27

12. Jacob caused the rise of his grandsons Manasseh and Ephraim by naming his name over them.

The Angel which redeemed me from all evil, bless the lads; and let my name be named on them, and the name of my fathers Abraham and Isaac; and let them grow into a multitude in the midst of the earth.

Genesis 48:16

13. Jacob caused the rise of his grandson Ephraim over his older brother, Manasseh by declaring that the younger would be greater than the older.

And his father refused, and said, I know *it*, my son, I know *it*: he also shall become a people, and he also shall be great: but truly his younger brother shall be greater than he, and his seed shall become a multitude of nations.

And he blessed them that day, saying, in thee shall Israel bless, saying, God make thee as Ephraim and as Manasseh: and he set Ephraim before Manasseh.

Genesis 48:19-20

14. A father causes the fall of sons by the release of ravens and eagles to pluck out the eyes of children who despise them.

The eye *that* mocketh at *his* father, and despiseth to obey *his* mother, the ravens of the valley shall pick it out, and the young eagles shall eat it."

Proverbs 30:17

15. Noah caused the fall of his son Canaan by cursing him to become a servant of servants.

And Noah awoke from his wine, and knew what his younger son had done unto him. And he said, Cursed *be* Canaan; a servant of servants shall he be unto his brethren.

Genesis 9:24-25

16. Jacob caused the fall of his son, Reuben, by declaring that he would not excel.

Reuben, thou *art* my firstborn, my might, and the beginning of my strength, the excellency of dignity, and the excellency of power:

Unstable as water, thou shalt not excel; because thou wentest up to thy father's bed; then defiledst thou it: he went up to my couch.

Genesis 49:3-4

17. Jacob caused the fall of his sons; Simeon and Levi, by declaring that they would be scattered.

Simeon and Levi *are* brethren; instruments of cruelty are in their habitations.... Cursed *be* their anger, for *it* was fierce; and their wrath, for it was cruel: I will divide them in Jacob, and scatter them in Israel.

Genesis 49:5,7

18. Isaac caused the fall of his son Esau by declaring that he would serve his brother.

And Isaac his father answered and said unto him, Behold, thy dwelling shall be the fatness of the earth, and of the dew of heaven from above;

And by thy sword shalt thou live, and shalt serve thy brother; and it shall come to pass when thou shalt have the dominion, that thou shalt break his yoke from off thy neck.

Genesis 27:39-40

His father, Isaac, said to him, "You will live off the land and what it yields, and you will live by your sword. You will serve your brother for a time, but then you will shake loose from him and be free."

Genesis 27:39-40 (NLT)

Chapter 13

Four Marks of a Father

Not every man of God is a father. There are pastors, apostles, teachers and evangelists who are not fathers. On the other hand, there are pastors, teachers, evangelists and apostles who are fathers.

Any of these callings can take on the cloak of fatherhood. Fatherhood adds an extra dimension of love to whichever calling of ministry you have.

1. A father has the ability to produce sons and daughters.

The cardinal sign of a father is not his age. Unfortunately, most people equate old age to fatherhood. The opposite is true. Most of us became fathers when we were young and in our twenties.

We develop and perfect the art of fathering as we grow older. The cardinal sign of a father is his ability to produce offspring. A classic example of this truth is seen in the lives of the two prophets, Elijah and Elisha. Even though Elisha had a greater anointing than Elijah, he had neither successor nor son in the ministry. Elisha had earlier cursed the only son God had given him (Gehazi). Instead of Gehazi becoming a son in the ministry, he became a leprosy patient! Elisha had also cursed some little children for laughing at him. Apparently, he had no time for children.

The double portion of anointing on the prophet's life didn't transform him into a father.

2. A father has a large heart of forgiveness.

Notice how Elijah was deserted by his first servant but still took another servant (Elisha). He had the heart to try again.

**And the LORD said... go... and Elisha the son of
Shaphat of Abel-meholah shalt thou anoint to be
prophet in thy room.**

1 Kings 19:15-16

When Elisha disobeyed and refused to stay in Jericho, Jordan,
Gilgal or Bethel, Elijah did not become angry with Elisha and
curse him. Instead, he was open to Elisha's request for a double
portion of the anointing.

Men of God who don't become fathers often suffer from
idealism and perfectionism.

These are delusions that keep us from the grace of fatherhood.
No one is perfect and people with this delusion attack God's
children who are making an effort to improve.

People who cannot become fathers have no time for
imperfections and lapses. This delusion frustrates the grace of
God. God's grace helps us to climb the mountain until we reach
the peak of perfection. If God had to wait until we were perfect,
He would never be able to use any of us. None of the apostles
would have qualified under these conditions of perfection.

3. A father has a lot of patience.

Anyone who has a lot of patience will have a lot of children.
Fathers are able to wait for people to change and improve. A
father will be there when the change finally comes. Fathers have
space in their hearts for all sorts of people. They can see that
after several falls, a shining star will be born.

That is why the prodigal son's father called for the best robe
and for a ring to be brought out for the wretched returnee. Notice
how the elder brother, who had no fathering abilities, was angered
by the return of his brother!

The fathering heart has big latitude to accommodate all
sorts of excursions made by potential sons and daughters. If
our Heavenly father did not have this heart of love, which of us
would be a son today?

4. A father provides for his children.

This role of a father is seen in the Lord's Prayer, where we ask our Father to give us daily bread. We also ask Him to deliver us from evil and to help us. A real father helps and provides.

Receiving honour and gifts is not the main function of a father. It is the opposite. Providing for children is the main duty of a father.

If you are fortunate, some of your children will remember and honour you. Receiving honour and gifts is simply a privilege that you may or may not receive as a father.

Fathers must provide direction! Fathers must provide protection! Fathers must provide for the needs of their children.

Chapter 14

Twenty Reasons Why a Son Must Be an "Allos"

The purpose of having a son is to produce another person of the same kind as you. God's unique plan for sons is that they should be another of the same kind. Actually, God's unique plan for all creation is that all parents should bring forth species of the same kind.

There is an important Greek word *"Allos"* which means *"another of the same kind"*. This is in sharp contrast to *"heteros"* which means "another of a different kind". Heteros is used to describe something or someone who is similar but a little different.

One of the strong delusions of sons is the delusion that, "I am something special, new and original that the world has been waiting for." The deception is that "I am better than my fathers and I am going to do something very different from what the fathers could do."

But our aim must be to love the Lord and to do whatever He wants us to do.

Our aim must not be to be special or unique in any way. We must desire to learn from the fathers God has put in front of us.

Why do you despise everything your father stands for? Why do you want to be so different and so special? Is it not the pride of life that drives this need to be totally different from everyone ahead of you? I have come to see that I am not different from any other minister. I am not some rare species whom Christ has chosen for the end-time move. Such thoughts only lead to error. I am a member of the Lord's army. I am so glad to be one of the many who are trying to serve the Lord.

Do you want to be a teacher in the house of the Lord? God has been raising up teachers for many years. If God is going to give you a teaching gift, you will simply be another teacher of the same kind. Do you want to raise up a great church? Don't start your ministry in deception. Your church will simply be another church of the same kind.

Thoughts of being unique and totally different from everything that has existed before, only leads to delusions. It is time to learn from fathers who stand right before you. God wants to raise up more shepherds like the fathers of old. Shepherds who humbly received and learnt from experienced fathers!

I use the word "allos" to mean another of the same kind. I believe that sons must aspire to be at least another of the same kind. There are many good things about your father and you can at least learn those good things and perhaps do even better.

1. **A son must be an allos because it is GOD'S PLAN as revealed in the creation.**

   And God said, Let us make man in our image, after our likeness...

   Genesis 1:26

When the Lord created man, he created something that was like Himself. He said that let us make something that is like us: another of the same kind. We were all created as alloses.

There are many similarities between man and God because we are made in His image. God is a Spirit and the Father of spirits. Human beings are also spirits living in bodies. God the Father, God the Son and God the Holy Spirit make up the Trinity we know.

Man as spirit, soul and body also makes up a triune being. When men walk in their creative and inventive elements they are clearly exhibiting the likeness of God. Allos: another of the same kind!

2.   A son must be an allos because it is A GOOD THING.

And the earth brought forth grass, and herb yielding seed after his kind... and God saw that it was good. And God created... every living creature ... after their kind... and God saw that it was good. And God made the beast of the earth after his kind... and God saw that it was good.

Genesis 1:12, 21, 25

So God created man in his own image, in the image of God created he him; male and female created he them. And God saw every thing that he had made, and, behold, it was very good...

Genesis 1:27, 31

It is a good *thing* to be another of the same kind. Almighty God created things to produce after their kind. The grass produces another of the same kind, the herbs produce another of the same kind, and the whales produce another of the same kind. Even man produces another of the same kind.

The Lord God saw that another of the same kind was a good thing! Instead of being preoccupied with producing another of a *different* kind, let us do what is good.

Do you want to be a good singer? Aim at something you can achieve. Desire something that you can lay hold on. Desire to be an allos of someone who is already a great singer.

3.   A son must be an allos because everyone is an allos of someone else.

If you are not an allos of your father you will be an allos of someone else. People who claim they are not following anyone are simply following someone they have not acknowledged. Everyone that is great in ministry is an allos of someone else. Everyone who is a great worship leader is an allos of some worship leader somewhere. Everyone who is a great evangelist is an allos of another evangelist. Every great man of God is an allos of some man of God somewhere.

Every anointing is the allos of another anointing. The anointing that came on Peter, James and John was simply an allos of the anointing that was on Jesus their master. The anointing that was on Elisha was simply another of the same kind of what was on Elijah.

Recently, I was having breakfast in a hotel in South Africa. Here came a famous Christian singer whose music and CDs were played all over the world. As we sat together, one of my pastors, Pastor Oko asked him a question, "Who has influenced you in your music ministry?"

He answered, "Oh, Andrae Crouch has been my greatest inspiration."

I immediately understood why this fellow was doing so well. He was a shameless allos! He was proud to be another of the same kind.

I have noticed that all those who do well in any field, are alloses who closely follow after someone of the same kind. Whether it is preaching, singing, healing, or to pastor, the principle is the same. God is producing another of the same kind and He continually says that it is a good thing.

4. It is a good thing that a son must be an allos because it makes him humble.

It is a good thing to be an allos because it is a humble thing!

It is a good thing to have to humbly learn from those ahead of you.

It is a good thing for the young to show respect to those who have made a way for them.

When sons are humble, the blessings of God pass on to the next generation. Not only will there be one great man of God for this generation, but there will be another of the same kind for the next generation.

Not only will there be one great singer, but many of the same kind. Everywhere those gifted voices are needed to help the anointing flow, there will be an allos.

5. A son must become an allos because it will make him a great person.

Decide to be a great man of God; decide to become a great worship leader. Become a choir leader or a shepherd people will not forget. How can you do this? The answer is simple: become another of the same kind. Let us not become mystical about the formula to greatness in God.

Let us not beat about the bush. Let's go directly to God's method of producing another of the same kind. If it is great, another of the same kind will also be great. If it is anointed, another of the same kind will be anointed. If it is powerful, another of the same kind will be powerful.

I believe that God has called me to serve Him. I am not special and I am not different. I am simply another of the kind that God has raised up already. I want to find someone with a similar calling and follow hard after him.

It won't be long and we will be going home. I don't have much time for trial and error. I cannot afford any time for experiments. I may be in the middle of an experiment when the Lord calls me.

I need to get straight to the point. I need the anointing and I need it fast! I need to preach well and I need to preach well now! I need to heal the sick and to raise the dead and I want it to happen within the time the Lord has given me.

How about you? How many years of experimentation are you going to dabble with until you become humble enough to become another of the same kind?

Churches that work are pastored by pastors of a certain kind.

Churches that grow are pastored by men and women of a certain kind. Since that is also your vision, why don't you become another of the same kind?

Allos is the way to the anointing. Allos is the key to greatness in God. Allos is the open door for you to enter the things of the kingdom.

I cannot pretend. What I do is what I have learnt from others. What I teach is what has been taught by another of the same kind. How I minister is what I learnt from someone else.

I have no shame about pressing hard after others of the same kind. God said it was good so it must be very good. If it is good for God, it is good for me.

6. A son must become an allos because there is nothing new under the sun.

When you become an allos, you discover the truth that there is nothing new under the sun.

The thing that hath been, it is that which shall be; and that which is done is that which shall be done: and there is no new thing under the sun. Is there any thing whereof it may be said, See, this is new? It hath been already of old time, which was before us.

Ecclesiastes 1:9-10

Indeed, there is nothing new under the sun. This is a fact that you must accept. You have nothing new to offer and your life will not really introduce anything special.

Like most ministers, I once thought I was introducing something new. I thought I had some new gifts and ideas, which no one else had ever had.

With time, I discovered that all that I was doing had been done before. Every single thing I am doing and saying I have found people who said them before I did.

The truth about my ministry is that I am simply following hard after others I genuinely admire. I want to be like them and I am not ashamed to say so! I like their spirit! I like their flow!

If I can be another of the same kind, I think it would be a great achievement for me.

7. A son must become an allos because you become something that is already SUCCESSFUL AND WORKING.

You are free from the disadvantage of experimentation. You are free from years of wasting time as you discover principles that have worked over and over again.

8. A son must become an allos because it saves you from the difficulty of having to create a new name.

Making a name is not easy. That is why names are sold for lots of money. A good name is one of the most valuable things on earth. Becoming another of the same kind means you are another with the same kind of name. When you do not mind the association, you can truly benefit from being an allos.

9. A son must become an allos because it makes you understand your place in the team.

It takes humility to admit that you are just part of a team. When people are impressed with your ministry, it is not easy to reveal that your message is not original. When people are impressed with your style it is not easy to reveal that you learnt everything from someone else. Thank God for the humility that becoming an allos gives.

And herein is that saying true, One soweth, and ANOTHER (ALLOS) reapeth.

John 4:37

When people of the same kind work together, it is possible to truly play as a team: "One soweth and another reapeth". When people are not of the same kind, it is very difficult to work together. Conflicts in church leadership are caused when people with different visions work together.

If I have ambitions for wealth, my decisions will be different from someone who has ambitions for bearing fruit. There will be continuous conflict because we are of different kinds.

Transferring pastors from one church to another is much easier when pastors of the same kind work together. When another of the same kind takes over a church, there is great encouragement for the church.

Both pastors realize they are transitional servants of the Lord with a "limited lease period" in which to please the Lord. No one is there forever and no one is there for personal gain. Each pastor wants to do his best for the Lord in his season. One plants the church, and another of the same kind waters it. Because they are of the same kind, they all recognize when it is time for the change. However such changes in church structure do not work where there are people with different ambitions.

Paul and Apollos were alloses: they were of the same kind.

According to the grace of God which is given unto me, as a wise masterbuilder, I have laid the foundation, and another (ALLOS) buildeth thereon. But let every man take heed how he buildeth thereupon

1 Corinthians 3:10

Paul did not mind laying a foundation for another to build upon. He did not mind starting up and allowing someone else to continue the work. Paul planted the church and another of the same kind (Apollos) watered it. When you are an allos you will understand that you are just part of a team.

10. A son must become an allos because it makes you dependent and sheep-like.

The sheep nature is different from the serpent nature. It is the nature of snakes to be independent and solitary. This is the very opposite of how you must be if you want to walk with the Lord. To be another of the same kind, you will have to depend on someone, you will have to learn from someone and you will have to follow someone.

11. A son must become an allos because it gives you access to methods and formulae that have worked for your kind.

When I decide to become another of the same kind, all I need are the methods which are used by my allos. What worked for him will work for me. I simply copy the systems and techniques that have produced results in my allos. Since I am going to be the same kind, the same kind of methods that worked for him will surely work for me!

12. A son must become an allos because it makes him a member of a particular group.

A unique group of people who are of the same kind, have many things in common. You can now fellowship freely because you have similar challenges and similar experiences. Whenever I meet allos pastors, I can relax and enjoy their company. I can share my challenges and be encouraged by others with similar experiences.

13. A son must become an allos because that is how you will find your way in the ministry.

Many who are called to the ministry do not know how to walk the road of ministry. They know God has called them but don't have a clue as to how to progress. Many men of God do not know how to climb into higher heights in ministry. They see other men of God accomplishing great things but don't know that they can do the same!

The road to accomplishing the same things is clear now. Don't try to be unique, special or different. Just become an allos. Become another of the same kind.

Use the techniques they used.

Follow them very closely.

Preach what they preached.

Pray in the same way that they prayed.

Seek God in the same way that they did.

Have the kind of close relationship with God. You will surely become another of the same kind.

14. A son must become an allos because it helps you to move faster into new areas of ministry.

Becoming an allos quickens your rate of advancement in life and ministry. Because you are following a well-chartered road, you have the benefit of those who went on before you.

You will not be slowed down by the things that slowed others down. You will overcome obstacles faster because your kind will give you tips on how to overcome them.

People go faster when they do not have to experiment with things.

One day, I was going somewhere with someone. He was in his car ahead and I was in mine. When he got into traffic, he called me and told me not to come the way he had gone because there was too much traffic. I ended up getting there faster than he did because he saved me from having to go through his problem. It is common sense to receive inputs from someone just ahead of you. Becoming an allos is actually the art of using common sense.

15. A son must become an allos because it will help you when you encounter difficulties.

Have you ever wondered why doctors are calm in the face of apparent emergencies? It is because they have seen many other situations of the same kind (allos). When you meet an allos problem or crisis, you are calm because you know this kind. You overcome it faster because you have been taught about this kind of situation.

16. A son must become an allos because an army of multiplied force is created thereby.

The joint effort of people of the same kind produces greater results. Bible teaches that two are better than one. It goes on to say that a threefold cord is not easily broken.

And if one prevail against him, two shall withstand him; and a threefold cord is not quickly broken.

Ecclesiastes 4:12

Two of the same kind are better than one! Three of the same kind, are not easily broken. The multiplied strength of allos is phenomenal. When people of the same mind walk and work together, great power is released.

How should one chase a thousand, and two put ten thousand to flight...

Deuteronomy 32:30

One of a kind shall put to flight a thousand but two of the same kind shall put to flight ten thousand.

17. A son must become an allos because that is the natural way to increase.

The natural way that all of creation multiplies is by producing another of the same kind.

And the earth brought forth grass, and herb yielding seed after his kind...and God saw that it was good. And God created...every living CREATURE...after their KIND...and God saw that it was good. And God made the beast of the earth after his kind...and God saw that it was good.

Genesis 1:12, 21, 25

The natural way that the church will grow from glory to glory is to produce pastors of the same kind, leaders of the same kind, and shepherds of the same kind. I do not dispute that there are other ways to move forward. But I can share what I see in the Bible. Allos! Allos! Allos! I want to be like the fathers God has given me. I want to be exactly like Him.

Herein is our love made perfect, that we may have boldness in the day of judgment: because as he is, so are we in this world.

1 John 4:17

18. A son must become an allos because it is the key to the anointing.

And I will pray the Father, and he shall give you another (ALLOS) Comforter, that he may abide with you for ever;

John 14:16

In the Scripture above, Jesus calls the Comforter, another of the same kind. The word another in this verse, is the Greek word allos. This means another comforter of the same kind. Jesus could have used the word heteros which would also have been translated another. But heteros would have meant a help of a different kind.

The Holy Spirit (Comforter) is the anointing. When Jesus promised another comforter of the same kind, He was promising another anointing of the same kind. The same kind of anointing with which He had ministered would be available to the apostles.

Most pastors would hasten their progress in the ministry if they would understand this simple truth. There is no new and special anointing that God wants to give you. He is simply going to give you another of the same kind. Even the apostles were promised another of the same kind.

The world's system teaches that the way to be qualified is to go to school. But the biblical pattern of becoming anything in the ministry is to become an allos. Becoming an allos is the natural way by which God produces ministers. Pride and presumption often keep us from becoming alloses.

The ministry is a very difficult thing. It takes a lot of grace to even please God. Humility is the greatest achievement in the ministry, yet it is so elusive. Most of us follow after human indicators of greatness. But Christ has shown what true greatness is. To humbly follow a man, to be obedient and to bear fruit in humility is no mean task. God does not require much from us. He expects us to become an allos of something that is working.

Elijah, Elisha and John-the-Baptist

Elijah had two well-known alloses: Elisha and John the Baptist. The Bible is clear on this fact. Elisha asked for a double portion of the anointing that was on Elijah and he got it (2 Kings 2:9). Jesus described John the Baptist as Elijah. He actually said, "This is Elias, which was for to come" (Matthew 11:14).

Whenever you have another of the same kind of anointing, it produces the same kind of works. A closer look at the ministries of these two alloses will show you how true this is. This revelation should inspire you to get an allos anointing.

Six Reasons Why Elisha Was an Allos of Elijah

1. Elijah prayed for the bringing back to life of a little boy (1 Kings 17:17-24) and Elisha also prayed for the raising up of a dead boy (2 Kings 4:32-37).

2. Elijah made miraculous utterances (1 Kings 21:28-29) and Elisha also made miraculous utterances (2 Kings 8:12).

3. Elijah had sixteen miracles in his ministry whilst Elisha had thirty-two miracles in his ministry.

4. Elijah caused a famine for three and a half years (1 Kings 17:1; James 5:17) and Elisha also prayed and there was a famine for seven years (2 Kings 8:1-2).

5. Elijah multiplied the meal and oil for a widow (1 Kings 17:8-16) and John the Baptist also increased the oil of a widow (2 Kings 4:1-7).

6. Elijah dried up the river Jordan (2 Kings 2:8) and John also dried up the river Jordan (2 Kings 2:13-15).

Eleven Reasons Why John the Baptist Was an Allos of Elijah

1. Elijah was anointed with the Spirit and power (2 Kings 1:9-10) and John the Baptist was also filled with the Spirit and with power (Luke 1:17).

2. Elijah lived in the desert at a point (1 Kings 1:17:3, 19:4) whilst John the Baptist was also known to dwell in the wilderness (Luke 1:80).

3. Elijah had a peculiar appearance (2 Kings 1:8) whilst John the Baptist was also known to dress in camel skirt (Matthew 3:4).

4. Elijah ate strange food from the mouth of ravens (1 Kings 17:4) whilst John the Baptist ate locusts and wild honey (Matthew 3:4).

5. Elijah confronted the king of his day, King Ahab (1 Kings 18:17-18) and John the Baptist also confronted the ruler of his day, King Herod (Matthew 14:3-4).

6. The king desired to kill Elijah (2 Kings 1:9) and the king sought to kill John the Baptist also (Matthew 14:3-5).

7. Elijah preached righteousness (1 kings 18:20-24) and John the Baptist's main message was repentance (Matthew 21:32).

8. Elijah was hated by the king's wife, Jezebel (1 Kings 19:1-7) and John the Baptist was also hated by Herod's wife (Matthew 14:3-10).

9. Elijah was very influential in the land (1 Kings 18:25-41) and John the Baptist also had great influence in the land in his day (Mark11:32).

10. Elijah and John the Baptist were linked in prophecy (Malachi 3:1; Malachi 4:5-6; Isaiah 40:3).

11. Elijah will be the forerunner to the second coming of Christ (Malachi 4:5-6) and John the Baptist was the forerunner to the first coming of Christ (Malachi 3:1).

19. A son must become an allos because it is the key to the art of teaching and preaching.

Hear another [ALLOS] parable: There was a certain householder, which planted a vineyard, and hedged it round about, and digged a winepress in it, and built a tower, and let it out to husbandmen, and went into a far country:

Matthew 21:33

Jesus taught the Word of God in the most beautiful and anointed style ever known to man. His stories are remembered by little children long after they stop reading the Bible. His teachings are relevant two thousand years after He gave them.

The teachings of Jesus are read by more people, quoted by more authors, translated into more languages, set to more music and represented in more art than any other teachings.

As someone said, comparing the teachings of Socrates, Plato and Aristotle to those of Jesus is like comparing an enquiry with a revelation!

Years ago, I told my beloved that I wanted to be a teacher of the Word like Jesus. I thought to myself, "The teachings of Jesus are not easily forgotten, even by children." I decided to become an allos. Years ago, before I became a pastor, I decided to teach and preach with stories. Jesus told so many stories. He would say:

"A *certain man* had two sons…"

"A *certain man* made a great party…"

"There was a *certain rich* man which was clothed in purple…"

"A *certain rich man* died…"

"A *certain man* went up from Jericho..."

"There was a *certain rich man* which had a steward..."

"The ground of a *certain rich man* brought forth bountifully..."

"A *certain noble man* went into a far country..."

I decided that I wanted to be a teacher like Jesus. I didn't want to be anything new; I just wanted to be an allos.

The key to becoming a great preacher is to become another of the same kind. Just find a preacher whose ministry touches lives and become another of the same kind. Learn how to preach by becoming the same as he is. Preach in the same way, teach in the same way and you will be very successful. Don't try anything new because there is nothing new.

Learn how to honourably "copy, photocopy, photograph, replay, rewind, repeat" what is good until it becomes a part of you. You will find yourself becoming an allos. The reality is that whether you do this deliberately or not, you are becoming the allos of somebody. So why not choose to become the allos of somebody you admire?

20. A son must become an allos because it will help him to recognize the principle of allos in many other areas of ministry.

When you understand the principle of allos you understand that it is at work in many areas of life and ministry. Just as you are another of the same kind, you will recognize that many things are just one of a kind.

Dear friend, there is nothing special about you. There is nothing special about the problems you encounter in ministry. Someone has experienced it before and you are just the next one to discover it.

In the book of Revelation, John saw a terrible beast (problem) rising out of the sea. He was amazed at the strange and frightening appearance of this beast.

And I stood upon the sand of the sea, and saw a beast rise up out of the sea, having seven heads and ten horns, and upon his horns ten crowns, and upon his heads the name of blasphemy. And the beast which I saw was like unto a leopard, and his feet were as the feet of a bear, and his mouth as the mouth of a lion: and the dragon gave him his power, and his seat, and great authority.

Revelation 13:1-2

But this was not the end. He suddenly saw an allos! Another of the same kind! The Scripture describes how he saw another beast of the same kind emerging from beneath the ocean.

And I beheld another (ALLOS) beast coming up out of the earth; and he had two horns like a lamb, and he spake as a dragon.

Revelation 13:11

It is important to recognize problems of a similar nature when they arise. This will help you to calmly deal with the problems.

I once preached at a church in which the people were really blessed. The pastor of the church was also happy with the message. However, a few days later, this pastor told me that he was not happy about certain things I had said in his church. I was taken aback because he had initially said that he was very happy with the message.

This pastor continued to take up the issue, explaining that certain people among his pastors and congregation were not happy with my preaching. I came to realize that there was a political spirit at work in that congregation. The church was run on the strength of rumours, criticism and gossip. The different groups and factions always had an opinion about what was going on in the church. It was a church fraught with division, politics and infighting.

On another occasion, I preached in another church elsewhere. After the message, the pastor was very happy and congratulated me. He went on to say that he would have liked me to preach that very same message in his church at a larger Sunday service. He wanted the whole church to hear it. But I explained that I would not be available for that service.

The next day however, this pastor called me up and rebuked me for things that I had said in the message. I was taken aback but I apologized immediately for the wrong things that I had said. He explained that after I left, some of his leaders had voiced their objection to parts of my message

But I had already noticed similarities between this church and the other political church I had been in. I was therefore not too surprised by what had happened. It was an allos of the other political church where I had also been rebuked for my preaching. I was just having another of the same kind of experience. The pool of Siloam was surrounded by ill people with similar problems.

The impotent man answered him, Sir, I have no man, when the water is troubled, to put me into the pool: but while I am coming, another (ALLOS) steppeth down before me.

John 5:7

Chapter 15

Why Some Sons Find It Difficult To Honour Fathers

Honour thy father and mother; (which is the first commandment with promise;) That it may be well with thee, and thou mayest live long on the earth.

Ephesians 6:2-3

Honour thy father and thy mother: that thy days may be long upon the land which the Lord thy God giveth thee.

Exodus 20:12

1. **People find it difficult to honour fathers because they are not following Jesus Christ .**

Jesus Christ was preceded by John the Baptist. John the Baptist was in the ministry before Jesus came along. The Lord honoured him greatly, submitting Himself to him for baptism. This is exactly what many ministers cannot do. They do not honour the people that are ahead of them, especially if they live in the same city.

Seven Reasons Why Jesus Could Have Despised John the Baptist

1. Jesus had good reasons not to honour John the Baptist. Jesus Christ was the Son of God. Jesus Christ was in the beginning and all things were made by Him and through Him. John the Baptist was just another of God's creatures. How could Jesus Christ the creator bow down or submit himself to a mere human?

2. John the Baptist was not worthy to even untie the shoelaces of Jesus, much less to baptise Him.

And as the people were in expectation, and all men mused in their hearts of John, whether he were the Christ, or not;

John answered, saying unto *them* all, I indeed baptize you with water; but one mightier than I cometh, the latchet of whose shoes I am not worthy to unloose: he shall baptize you with the Holy Ghost and with fire:

Whose fan *is* in his hand, and he will throughly purge his floor, and will gather the wheat into his garner; but the chaff he will burn with fire unquenchable.

Luke 3:15-17

3. John's lifestyle was questionable. He wore skimpy panties to preach and lived in the desert.

In those days came John the Baptist, preaching in the wilderness of Judaea,

And saying, Repent ye: for the kingdom of heaven is at hand.

For this is he that was spoken of by the prophet Esaias, saying, The voice of one crying in the wilderness, Prepare ye the way of the Lord, make his paths straight.

And the same John had his raiment of camel's hair, and a leathern girdle about his loins; and his meat was locusts and wild honey.

Then went out to him Jerusalem, and all Judaea, and all the region round about Jordan, and were baptized of him in Jordan, confessing their sins.

Matthew 3:1-6

4. John the Baptist seemed to be delving into politics and was in direct confrontation with the government of the day.

5. John the Baptist's ministry had ended abruptly with him being executed like a common criminal.

   But Jesus respected John the Baptist. He acknowledged him and went to his church. Jesus submitted Himself to the ministry of John the Baptist.

Then cometh Jesus from Galilee to Jordan unto John, to be baptized of him. But John forbad him, saying, I have need to be baptized of thee, and comest thou to me? And Jesus answering said unto him, Suffer it to be so now: for thus it becometh us to fulfil all righteousness. Then he suffered him.

Matthew 3:13-15

6. John the Baptist did not have a miracle ministry. Jesus spoke highly of John the Baptist even though He did miracles which John the Baptist didn't do.

And as they departed, Jesus began to say unto the multitudes concerning John, What went ye out into the wilderness to see? A reed shaken with the wind? But what went ye out for to see? A man clothed in soft raiment? behold, they that wear soft clothing are in kings' houses. But what went ye out for to see? A prophet? yea, I say unto you, and more than a prophet. For this is he, of whom it is written, Behold, I send my messenger before thy face, which shall prepare thy way before thee.

Matthew 11:7-10

7. John the Baptist did not have powerful teachings like Jesus. Jesus preached a different kind of message from John but acknowledged the greatness and relevance of John the Baptist.

Verily I say unto you, Among them that are born of women there hath not risen a greater than John the Baptist: notwithstanding he that is least in the kingdom of heaven is greater than he.

Matthew 11: 11

After Jesus had submitted Himself to the ministry of John the Baptist, a voice from Heaven said, "This is my beloved son in whom I am well pleased." Jesus had not won any souls when He received this appellation –"this is my beloved son"! All He did was to submit Himself to someone ahead of Him in ministry. This is an important point for those who love to fight anything older or bigger than they are.

2. People find it difficult to honour fathers because they do not follow the example of King David.

King David acknowledged Saul as being the anointed king before him. Even though Saul had many problems, David did not attack him. He called him "father". David did not call Saul "the mad man of Jerusalem". He called him the Lord's anointed. He did not call him the "demonized king"or "demonized daddy". That is why his throne of David will be established forever.

He shall be great, and shall be called the Son of the Highest: and the Lord God shall give unto him the throne of his father David:

Luke 1:32

There are four things about Saul that would have driven any normal son to rebel against his father. But not David, he knew better. He knew the verse in Exodus 20:12; that his longevity depended on how he related to the fathers.

David Had Four Reasons Not to Honour Saul

1. Saul was rejected by God through the prophet Samuel.

...Because thou hast rejected the word of the LORD, he hath also rejected thee from being king.

1 Samuel 15:23b

2. Saul was demon-possessed. He came under the influence of evil spirits and David knew it.

And it came to pass on the morrow, that the evil spirit from God came upon Saul, and he prophesied in the midst of the house: and David played with his hand, as at other times: and there was a javelin in Saul's hand.

1 Samuel 18:10

3. Saul killed pastors. He had become a murderer and his victims were none other than God's priests.

And Abiathar shewed David that Saul had slain the LORD's priests.

1 Samuel 22:21

4. Saul was into witchcraft. His last night on earth was spent in a witch's house.

Then said Saul unto his servants, Seek me a woman that hath a familiar spirit, that I may go to her, and enquire of her. And his servants said to him, Behold, there is a woman that hath a familiar spirit at Endor.

1 Samuel 28:7

In spite of great provocation, David maintained his stance toward Saul. He refused to see him as anything other than a father. There are many ignoramuses who launch furious attacks against fathers because of the faults they see in them. Why not learn from David whose throne is established forever? Surely you do not have more good reasons than David did, to rebel against a father!

Moreover, my father, see, yea, see the skirt of thy robe in my hand: for in that I cut off the skirt of thy robe and killed thee not, know thou and see that there is neither evil nor transgression in mine hand, and I have not sinned against thee; yet thou huntest my soul to take it.

1 Samuel 24:11

3. **People find it difficult to honour fathers because their hearts are TURNED AWAY from their fathers.**

    And he shall turn the heart of the fathers to the children, and the heart of the children to their fathers, lest I come and smite the earth with a curse.

                                                    Malachi 4:6

There is a time when sons are not interested in what their fathers do. These sons are interested in the exact opposite of whatever their fathers desire. This is a condition that leads to a curse. There are many examples of this.

For instance, if a father is a university lecturer, the son may say in his heart, "I do not want to be a university lecturer." If the father is a politician and the heart of the son is turned away from his father, the son may grow up secretly deciding never to have anything to do with politics.

Similarly, the father may be a pastor in the ministry and the son will say things like, "I want to be a lawyer or an astronaut but not a pastor." All these are as a result of the hearts of the children being turned away from the father.

It is important to pray for your child so that his heart will be turned to his father. When children's' hearts are turned away from their fathers, they become independent and rebellious.

The Pastor's Daughter

Once, I was with a pastor's family and I got to talking with his daughter. As I chatted with her, she related how she was studying for her law degree. Her plans were for a corporate job in the corporate world. Meanwhile, her father was pastoring a great church with thousands of people but she had no interest in what he was doing.

A couple of years later, I came back to that city and was chauffeured around by this same pastor's daughter. This time all she talked about was the ministry. I wondered where her legal dreams had disappeared to. There was no more talk of the corporate world. It was just God and His work.

So I told her, "You have changed! I think a real change has come over you in relation to God and the ministry." So I asked again, "Have you changed?"

She responded, "Yes, I have."

I told her, "I noticed it the moment I interacted with you. The last time I was here, you were very different from what you are now."

She nodded, "That's true."

Then she confessed to me, "I have always wanted to stay away from ministry life. Our family suffered so much because of the ministry and I never wanted to be in it. I can't even understand why I have changed so much."

She added, "I am scared of my new interest in ministry. All I want to do is to travel with my father and help him in the ministry."

But I understood what had happened to her. God had turned the heart of the child towards the father to avoid a curse. The turning of the heart is a spiritual thing and only God can do it. It is important for parents to pray for their children otherwise their hearts will be turned away from all that is good and recommended by parents.

Turning the Father's Heart

There are also times when the father loses interest in his sons. This usually happens when the father is hurt or disillusioned with his children. It brings a curse on the children because they are left without any fatherly input.

One day, one of my lay pastors who had been out of the country for some years came home. Before he left the country, he confided in another pastor. He said, "I think the Bishop has lost interest in some of us." I just feel that he is not as interested in us as he used to be."

I was surprised that he was able to quickly pick that up because he was right. I had been so disillusioned and disappointed in some of the pastors that I had lost interest in them. I wouldn't call them for meetings and I wouldn't say much to them. I would just smile to everyone and say, "You are blessed!" But I wouldn't engage in a deep and substantial discussion with any of them. You see, my heart had turned away from these pastors.

But God began to turn my heart back to them. He made me pray for them and gradually, I regained the love and interest for these pastors. I then understood first-hand what it meant for the heart of the father to be turned away from his children. It is indeed a dangerous thing and it does bring a curse. Pray that your father's heart will not be turned away from you.

4. People find it difficult to honour fathers because they feel a father must earn their honour by being honourable.

Unfortunately, many sons and daughters are disappointed in the lives of their fathers and mothers. They are often disappointed at the marriages of their parents.

Many sons think they will do better than their parents have done with money, relationships and other opportunities of life. Some children even think they will look after their own children better than their parents looked after them.

It is true that most parents fall short of the ideal father and mother. Every parent is a phantom of what he could be. Parents are just human beings. Fathers are easy to criticize because their lives are out in the open.

It is also true that an "imperfect" father may bring a "perfect" man into the world and a good person may bring an evil person into the world. For instance, Hitler and Stalin had mothers who took them to church. Both Hitler and Stalin were members of the choirs in their churches.

Stalin even attended a bible school for a period. Obviously, the parents of these mass murderers were Christians and churchgoers. Somehow they brought forth men who would cause the deaths of millions of people.

God knows that many of the parents of "good" people are not "good". And yet, He gave a blanket instruction that fathers and mothers should be honoured. This scripture presents itself as a hurdle or a stumbling block to many who would have excelled in life and ministry.

The obvious moral, financial and marital failings of fathers have nothing to do with the honour that God has commanded us to give to them. If God wants to punish the fathers for their financial, moral and marital sins, He will. That has nothing to do with the honour a child is expected to give to his father.

Remember the words of Jesus when He said, "give unto Caesar the things that belong to Caesar and unto God the things that are God's. Every father, no matter who he is, is due the honour commanded by God for him. God does not lose anything when Caesar receives the taxes that belong to him. That is why Jesus said that people should go ahead and give Caesar his taxes.

God's kingdom does not lose anything when fathers receive the honour that belong to them. The morals, the holiness and the righteousness of the kingdom of God will not be compromised when a father is honoured.

Many people are "over righteous", self righteous and judgmental when it comes to the sins of their fathers. They use the errors, the flaws and the obvious sins of their fathers as excuses to withhold the honour that is due them.

Like Pharisees, they see the commandments of God as mutually exclusive. In other words, you cannot maintain the moral standards and at the same time give honour to a father if he has committed any such sins.

If it were the case that only perfect fathers were to be honoured, then there would be no need of the fifth commandment (Honour thy father...) because there is no perfect father on this earth!

5.   People find it difficult to honour fathers because they add to the fifth commandment.

If you meditate on the fifth commandment, you will discover that it does not describe the type of mother or father you are supposed to honour. It simply says you are to honour your father and a mother. By adding to the scripture, they make it impossible to obey. Here are some examples of how people add to the fifth commandment:

a.   People find it difficult to honour fathers because they think the scripture says: 'Honour *thy father who is perfect* that it may be well with thee and thou mayest live long on the earth.'

But the Bible actually says: "Honour thy father and mother; ...that it may be well with thee, and thou mayest live long on the earth."

b.   People find it difficult to honour fathers because they think the scripture says: 'Honour t*hy father who is rich* that it may be well with thee and thou mayest live long on the earth.'

But the Bible actually says: "Honour thy father and mother; ...that it may be well with thee, and thou mayest live long on the earth."

c.   People find it difficult to honour fathers because they think the scripture says: 'Honour *thy father who was a good husband to your mother* that it may be well with thee and thou mayest live long on the earth.'

But the Bible actually says: "Honour thy father and mother; ...that it may be well with thee, and thou mayest live long on the earth."

d.   People find it difficult to honour fathers because they think the scripture says: 'Honour *thy father who paid your school fees* that it may be well with thee and thou mayest live long on the earth.'

But the Bible actually says: "Honour thy father and mother; ... that it may be well with thee, and thou mayest live long on the earth."

e.   People find it difficult to honour fathers because they think the scripture says: 'Honour *thy father who did not divorce your mother* that it may be well with thee and thou mayest live long on the earth.'

But the bible actually says: "Honour thy father and mother; ...that it may be well with thee, and thou mayest live long on the earth."

f.   People find it difficult to honour fathers because they think the scripture says: 'Honour *thy father who was married to only one wife* that it may be well with thee and thou mayest live long on the earth.'

But the Bible actually says: "Honour thy father and mother; ...that it may be well with thee, and thou mayest live long on the earth."

g.   People find it difficult to honour fathers because they think the scripture says: 'Honour *thy father who had children with only one woman* that it may be well with thee and thou mayest live long on the earth.'

But the Bible actually says: "Honour thy father and mother; ...that it may be well with thee, and thou mayest live long on the earth."

h.   People find it difficult to honour fathers because they think the scripture says: 'Honour *thy father who did not fall into sin* that it may be well with thee and thou mayest live long on the earth.'

But the Bible actually says: "Honour thy father and mother; ...that it may be well with thee, and thou mayest live long on the earth."

i.   People find it difficult to honour fathers because they think the scripture says: 'Honour *thy father who was always at home* that it may be well with thee and thou mayest live long on the earth.'

But the Bible actually says: "Honour thy father and mother; ...that it may be well with thee, and thou mayest live long on the earth."

j.   People find it difficult to honour fathers because they think the scripture says: 'Honour *thy father who built a house for the family* that it may be well with thee and thou mayest live long on the earth.'

But the Bible actually says: "Honour thy father and mother; ...that it may be well with thee, and thou mayest live long on the earth."

k.   People find it difficult to honour fathers because they think the scripture says: 'Honour t*hy father who left you an inheritance* that it may be well with thee and thou mayest live long on the earth.'

But the Bible actually says: "Honour thy father and mother; ...that it may be well with thee, and thou mayest live long on the earth."

l.   People find it difficult to honour fathers because they think the scripture says: 'Honour *thy father who related well with all his children* that it may be well with thee and thou mayest live long on the earth.'

But the Bible actually says: "Honour thy father and mother; ...that it may be well with thee, and thou mayest live long on the earth."

m.   People find it difficult to honour fathers because they think the scripture says: 'Honour *thy father who had no weaknesses* that it may be well with thee and thou mayest live long on the earth.'

But the Bible actually says: "Honour thy father and mother; ...that it may be well with thee, and thou mayest live long on the earth."

n.   People find it difficult to honour fathers because they think the scripture says: 'Honour *thy father who had a lot of money* that it may be well with thee and thou mayest live long on the earth.'

But the Bible actually says: "Honour thy father and mother; ...that it may be well with thee, and thou mayest live long on the earth."

o.   People find it difficult to honour fathers because they think the scripture says: 'Honour t*hy father who achieved a lot in his life* that it may be well with thee and thou mayest live long on the earth.'

But the Bible actually says: "Honour thy father and mother; ...that it may be well with thee, and thou mayest live long on the earth."

p.   People find it difficult to honour fathers because they think the scripture says: 'Honour *thy father who was a great man* that it may be well with thee and thou mayest live long on the earth.'

But the Bible actually says: "Honour thy father and mother; ...that it may be well with thee, and thou mayest live long on the earth."

q.   People find it difficult to honour fathers because they think the scripture says: 'Honour *thy father who played a great role in your life* that it may be well with thee and thou mayest live long on the earth.'

But the Bible actually says: "Honour thy father and mother; ...that it may be well with thee, and thou mayest live long on the earth."

r.   People find it difficult to honour fathers because they think the scripture says: 'Honour *thy father who accepted you as his son* that it may be well with thee and thou mayest live long on the earth.'

But the Bible actually says: "Honour thy father and mother; ...that it may be well with thee, and thou mayest live long on the earth."

s. People find it difficult to honour fathers because they think the scripture says: 'Honour *thy father who you lived with* that it may be well with thee and thou mayest live long on the earth.'

But the Bible actually says: "Honour thy father and mother; ...that it may be well with thee, and thou mayest live long on the earth."

t. People find it difficult to honour fathers because they think the scripture says: 'Honour *thy father who did not shout at you and rebuke you* that it may be well with thee and thou mayest live long on the earth.'

But the Bible actually says: "Honour thy father and mother; ...that it may be well with thee, and thou mayest live long on the earth."

u. People find it difficult to honour fathers because they think the scripture says: 'Honour *thy father who gave you a lot of money* that it may be well with thee and thou mayest live long on the earth.'

But the bible actually says: "Honour thy father and mother; ...that it may be well with thee, and thou mayest live long on the earth."

v. People find it difficult to honour fathers because they think the scripture says: 'Honour *thy father who was a born-again Christian* that it may be well with thee and thou mayest live long on the earth.'

But the Bible actually says: "Honour thy father and mother; ...that it may be well with thee, and thou mayest live long on the earth."

w.   People find it difficult to honour fathers because they think the scripture says: 'Honour *thy father who was not an illiterate* that it may be well with thee and thou mayest live long on the earth.'

But the Bible actually says: "Honour thy father and mother; ...that it may be well with thee, and thou mayest live long on the earth."

x.   People find it difficult to honour fathers because they think the scripture says: 'Honour t*hy father who was not into the occult* that it may be well with thee and thou mayest live long on the earth.'

But the Bible actually says: "Honour thy father and mother; ...that it may be well with thee, and thou mayest live long on the earth."

Indeed, honouring fathers and relating to fathers is truly a spiritual exercise. It may not make sense to the natural man but it is one of the greatest biblical principles of the Word of God.

Upon this fifth commandment, the entire human race rises and falls.

Upon this fifth commandment to honour your father and mother entire ministries rise and fall.

May you not struggle with the concept of honouring fathers!

May you be a good son so that one day you will be a good father!

May you honour others so that one day you will also receive honour!